A Year For Dad

Experiencing 1st Century Faith in the 21st Century

A. Berman

PublishAmerica
Baltimore

© 2009 by A. Berman.
All rights reserved. No part of this book may be reproduced, stored in a retrieval system or transmitted in any form or by any means without the prior written permission of the publishers, except by a reviewer who may quote brief passages in a review to be printed in a newspaper, magazine or journal.

First printing

PublishAmerica has allowed this work to remain exactly as the author intended, verbatim, without editorial input.

Copies of this book may be ordered in small or large quantities directly online from the publisher: http://www.publishamerica.net.

All scripture quotations, unless otherwise indicated, are taken from the Holy Bible, New International Version®, NIV®. Copyright ©1973, 1978, 1984 by Biblica, Inc.™ Used by permission of Zondervan. All rights reserved worldwide.

Scripture verses taken from The Message are Copyrighted © by Eugene H. Peterson, 1993, 1994, 1995. Used by permission of NavPress Publishing Group, Colorado Springs, CO.

Bible text from the Contemporary English Version (CEV) is reproduced in part by permission of the American Bible Society, 1865 Broadway, New York, NY 10023.

ISBN: 978-1-4489-9765-7
PUBLISHED BY PUBLISHAMERICA, LLLP
www.publishamerica.com
Baltimore

Printed in the United States of America

Dad is one of the most intense words I know.

To me, the very word DAD is synonymous with the distant memories of a guy I liked to be around, but never got to be around anywhere near as much as I wanted to be around. He was a man with a good sense of humor, and an ability to play. He appeared to be successful in his career, and he had a great poker face. He was also a die-hard Mets fan. Dad encouraged me to dream. A solid 50% of the time, he backed me at least 85% of the time. I think I inherited a lot of good stuff from him too. I'm grateful for that. Sometimes I get the impression that although physically trapped in his appointed time and place in history, he was really just a little ahead of his era.

It took me years to understand that my Dad loved me. All the expected trappings were there, but even today I still struggle with his dying and making me feel so left alone in the world. It was a time that a boy, or at least this boy, needed his father. Not really Dad's fault of course. He was just a guy who flew in and out of my life all too quickly. I know he was there. I have pictures. Somehow, someway, his blood is flowing through my veins today.

My perception of God, my Heavenly Father, bares a striking resemblance to the fellow I've been telling you about.

My dad was a man just like myself. I don't doubt that he wouldn't be too thrilled at being thrust into the position of representing The Creator of the Universe to his impressionable young son. Talk about pressure. I don't think he eve believed in God. The relationship parallels can be eerie though.

It's hard in this very distracting world to keep in my mind's forefront that I live in a very confusing and distracting world, one that my earthly father would have never understood. Whereas my Heavenly Father, has always been and always will be my Creator and my source of life. God loves me and that is unconditionally. He loves me with a passion so ferocious that He will do just about anything to get my attention, to get me to acknowledge His presence, to look Him in the eye, just to remind me who I am. I am His.

TABLE OF CONTENTS

Easter Eggs & Lifesavers 7
Bees 11
Puzzled 14
A Gaping Hole 18
Tough Cookie Training 22
Sweet Dreams 27
An Angel Named Gabe 32
God Knows 36
Love is Like That 40
Why God, Why? 45
One Day 48
Draw Near 52
Old Friends 56
Weapons of Mass Destruction 61
Mr. Nice Guy 65
Hard Candy Is Still Candy 69
Home Is Where The Heart Is 74
Heaven I Think. 78
Life Games 82
Shhh, Don't Tell 86
The Price of Admission 90
The Price of Admission: One Year Later 94
In The Twinkle of An Eye 97
NOTES & FOOTNOTES 102
THANKS & ACKNOWLEGEMENTS 105

Easter Eggs & Lifesavers

    I can clearly remember the old Lifesavers™ commercial that featured a very young Suzanne Sommers walking along the beach at sunrise, sharing a roll of breathmints with her aging Dad. At least I think it was a beach at sunrise. Maybe the memory is not so vivid, but the flavor of a child walking along life's path with Dad, discussing one of life's pleasant surprises, lingers. It lingers like the aftermath of a blast of Pep-O-Mint on your tongue on a warm summer day.
    I like to think that my Dad was a good guy. I have heard stories of some missteps, but other than that, word is, he was pretty ok. I was 15 when he died. He had cancer, and was undergoing chemo, but death was never really an option in my immature, pre-bipolar brain. I was away when it happened. I was working as an apprentice at a summer stock theatre in Danbury, Connecticut. It was not too far from home, although speeding through the murky, mid-summer night to find his empty, turned-down bed and a family in mournful shock seemed to take forever. My Dad's death was the single most earth-shaking event in my life. I wish I could say that my most transforming experience was when I found my way into God's loving arms through faith 3 years later, but that's really been more of an ongoing process than any kind of life-shattering explosion.
    My father's Will & Testament stated that he wanted no services, memorials or mourning. He wished life for those he loved to keep moving on as if nothing had happened. I used to think that this was one of the most noble things I'd ever heard. I'm starting to think that it was one of the most selfish things I've ever heard. My ex-wife taught me about the value of mourning. A buch of years later, on a cloudy

Monday afternoon, after I'd finished the appropriate amount of Pastoral visitation and paperwork, I decided to hijack my 150 seat sanctuary and have a long, overdue funeral service. It was cathartic. A dozen years had already passed, and still time would prove to be the greatest healer.

I'm almost 50 now. I've lived more than three times as long without him as I did with him. Seems like yesterday. Sometimes. I like to refer to my Dad poetically, as a phantom that slipped quietly, but profoundly, in and out of my life without me barely noticing. He is a sketchy character in my head. If I could go back in time, my Dad is the one contemporary person that I would most want to meet up with. Just for the record; that, and my suspicion that aliens are really time-travelers just about covers the extent of my sci-fi leanings. I have a few Father Knows Best memories, one in particular that brings a tear to my eye and a smile to my face every time I revisit it. I find, however, that it is the reality of his absence that has most acutely affected my image of a Father. I wish I'd had more time with him.

I can accept God's unconditional love, conditionally. Much of my Kingdom apprenticeship has been all about learning to receive His love, forgiveness and grace. When I'm listening, His lessons come through loud and clear. I do find, however, that The Big Guy Upstairs has no problem getting His point across when He really wants to. Eight and a half years in prison drove that lesson home for me quite clearly. Another big thing for me has been practicing the reality of God's Grace. Getting everything I don't deserve just because. It's really an amazing concept. Like a spiritual platinum American Express® card with no bill. It's the *NO MATTER WHAT Clause*... no matter what!

If I had three wishes, I think one of them would be to have a spiritual lobotomy. I would like very much to spend every hour of every day doing and saying stuff that doesn't make God roll His eyes at me. Aside from the obvious, I think one of the hardest parts about all of it is a principal that Jesus liked to talk about quite a bit: He who has been given much is responsible for much. (eg. Luke 16:10). I feel I have been given a lot. Out of all the craziness in my life has emerged a perspective that makes me grateful for even the most inconsequential of life's Easter eggs. Those colorful eggs you find hidden just about anywhere on Easter morning (and sometimes weeks following). I have been forgiven so very much, how can I not forgive everyone I meet, and give them a second and even third chance? And, I've learned to value honesty and faithfulness like gold. Ok, like chocolate. Godiva dark chocolate. The flip side is that I tend to daydream during some of life's most important lessons. I can be willful, disobedient, argumentative, lazy and irresponsible. It can be quite frustrating when I am trying to have a spiritual tantrum and the Lord comes galloping in on His white horse with all of that forgiveness, grace and love stuff. Sometimes, when I'm just complaining in prayer, I think, "if only my brain could be altered so that I do the stuff I want to do and don't do the stuff I know I shouldn't" (Romans 7:15-25).

The truth is, I don't think that mankind has even begun to understand the decimation of what happened at The Fall in the Garden of Eden (Genesis 3). And, I think that grasping hold of even the smallest understanding of the snare we are in helps to explain a lot of the mysteries that make people shake their fists at God. I should say too, that I believe that the Bible is 100% inspired by God. I think that if He cared enough to keep these writings around as long as they have been, it would be silly to allow the content to be compromised. I try to live my life on Jesus' clearly laid out Biblical principals. I don't however believe that everything people say that the Bible says, the Bible really says. I am what you would refer to as a *post-modernist*. Traditional church is one of the last places you will find me. If you do, I will undoubtedly be sweating and definitely hyperventilating. I urgently believe that God didn't set out a plan of salvation only for a people of only a certain time period. The simplicity of the Biblical times reference only once again shows His impeccable timing, even though the culture and language may be confusing to us. That's where faith and a personal relationship with Him come in. Today, I think that He reveals Himself, in contemporary ways, all the time. Everywhere. Usually where you least expect it.

What follows is for you, Dad. I've almost forgiven you for abandoning me at such a tender age, and for leaving me with just about enough life skills to cross the street without getting hit. When it comes right down to it, I think what almost any son wants from his Dad is approval. It's some kind of caveman right-of-passage thing. I never really had the chance to realize that, as far as I know. So, I've decided to share a year of my life with you; thirty-three years later. It's stuff I've experienced, lessons I'm learning, sometimes, just a written worksheet for figuring out one of life's mazes. Noel Coward might call it *journalesque*. Most importantly though, it's about how I am learning to be a child of God's in the 21st Century. A passion of mine that I think you would be respectfully proud of. Dad, the 21st Century is a time and place I wonder if you could have ever even dreamed of.

So Old Man, grab your fishin' pole. It's almost sunset and we're heading out to the lake…now I remember! Suzanne Sommers and her Dad were fishing on a lake at sunset. I don't think it's any coincidence that one Dad stepped in to my life just as the other stepped out. I do have a lot of questions though, being I'm a Dad now too. I'm hoping maybe this will turn some question marks into some exclamation points for me. It would be great too, if it could help someone else break free from the curse of 'the sins of the father' and see God for who He really is, despite what we've been told. Oddly, one of my first thoughts when hearing of someone's death is, "well, now it all makes sense to them." We live in a state that I would describe as muddy waters. God calls it the age of faith. I imagine that the process of death will be like diving into the murky waters of a scum-covered stagnant swamp and coming back up to the surface in to the crystal clearness of the Caribbean. I bethcha there's gonna be a lot of head slappin' going on. One day this is all going to make sense. I just know it is. (1 Corinthians 13:12,13). One thing is for sure, these three remain: faith, hope and love. But the greatest of these is love.

Bees

The weather has been extremely hot lately. Not just the kind of hot that makes you want to slip out of work early and head to the beach. The kind of hot that feels like you just got out of the shower when you are fully dressed. The other day, I decided to scrounge together all of my loose change and head out to the local recreation area. It's not the nicest lakefront I've ever seen; in fact it's usually pretty overcrowded with screaming kids and a head-banging combination of rap and salsa music fighting to out-deafen everyone there. The lake is fairly clean, the water is cool, and the view always makes me think about how much God likes to landscape. With my Bible and a can of Diet Coke® in tow, I found a fairly secluded area, took off my shirt, and strained to listen to the waves lapping at the shore.

Not long into my reverie, I began to realize that it wasn't the boom boxes polluting the air, but, in fact, a persistent buzzing. It was sort of like the sound you would hear watching a car race: soft to loud and then soft again. The first time I noticed it, I assumed a fly was craving some nutra-sweet from the sweating can at my side. When it happened over and over again, I started to get a little annoyed. Whatever little creature was performing maneuvers around my head obviously didn't realize that I was communing with our common Creator. I was sure that once I communicated how spiritual I was being at the moment he would realize his error, maybe apologize, and seek some barbequing family off in the distance to annoy. When I opened my eyes and sat up, all of my plans for détente came to a screaming halt. What I saw was what had to have been hundreds of gigantic bees hovering over the ground as if someone had poured honey all over the place. It was more than just a little overwhelming, but I reasoned that as long as I didn't mess with them maybe they wouldn't mess with me. After looking around and seeing that these herculean mutants were as far as the eye could see and far more interested in whatever was all over the ground than my puny collection of flesh and blood, I lay back down and got back to praying. The frenzied buzzing continued. I went swimming.

When I got home a few hours later I realized that that myriad of bees was very much like all of the things in life that distract me from the peace and sense of security that God wants me to experience every minute of every day. The life I should be living as opposed to the life that I am. In my minds eye, I laid back down on my wet towel at the lake and began naming those taunting little creatures: fear, self-pity, frustration, impatience, pride, lust, self-centeredness, hurt, jealousy, disappointment, on and on. It was Adam in the garden naming the animals all over again. Each and every one buzzing around my head, making me cringe, distracting my thoughts. The fascinating part about the whole experience was that as I lay resting in God's presence on both my real and imaginary towel, I didn't get bitten. Not even once. I was as safe as I could possibly be. I had to wonder, did God's venomous little creatures know that I was off limits, or did they only include me in their agendas when I included them in mine?

That night, I was reading about King David and his fling with Bathsheeba. Was that infamous night the first time he had ever been stung? What was he doing on the roof that night? Was he familiar with his neighbor's routine? Perhaps Israel's greatest King struggled with lust and pride more often throughout his life than is recorded. It also finally connected in my head that it was not any of his other children that succeeded him, it was Solomon, the son of the woman with whom he had fallen. The woman who's husband he had had killed and eventually married. The fruit of his most well-known failure.

The Apostle Paul writes in 2 Corinthians that he had a thorn in his flesh that, no matter how hard he prayed, wouldn't go away. He goes on to say that his greatest strength was actually his greatest weakness. As I struggle every day with my sin-stained humanity, I need to not just remember, but know that God is, in fact, intimately acquainted with all of my ways, that every one of my days was written in His book before one of them came to be (Ps. 139). It's okay to forgive myself when I do act human. I understand that God forgives me, but I feel like such a failure so much of the time. I see others around me winning victories, succeeding at life, out there loving as Christ loved, praying instead of reacting, appreciating life in all of it's glory instead of moaning about every raindrop. Not just believers either. Judging myself so harshly and beating myself up is not freedom. That sounds like bondage to me. If God knows and forgives me with such voracious love, aren't I just getting in His way when I override his generosity with my stinginess? Perhaps my self-berating is more pride than humility.

Life's bumble bees buzz around me from the minute I wake up in the morning to the minute I go to bed. Whether internally or externally, the minute I start waving them down is the minute I become part of their feeding frenzy. It's not the action of sin that robs my freedom, it's a matter of my heart refusing to rest in the all encompassing forgiveness of Christ that really stings. When I demand deliverance today but the Lord wants to transform my life in His time, aren't I in essence forgetting who is the Creator and who is the created? The blind man was over forty years old when Jesus healed him. Lazarus lay in the tomb for over three days before Jesus brought him back to life. In both cases, the Bible says that their situations existed so that God would be glorified (John 9:3; 11:4). Maybe those bees know something I don't. Their incessant buzzing did nothing but play with my head. When my attentions were directed heavenward they had no power over me. To be completely forgiven, truly loved, and totally surrendered to the purposes of my Maker, whether I understand it or not is the best bug spray of all. For the last few days, every time an insect has buzzed past my face, I can't help but smile. Bees are just as much a reminder to me of God's intimate participation in my life as a sunset, a starry night, or a breath-taking landscape framing a serene lake on a hot summer day.

Puzzled

    I had the privilege of watching a meteor shower last week. It was awesome. As I lay there on my back in the cool mid-August air, listening to the mystical sounds of summer, I couldn't help but wonder if God was showing off a little bit just for me. While my friend tried to explain the scientific ins and outs of all the heavenly pyrotechnics, I wondered if, although eloquently expressed, any words could possibly capture the profundity of what I was seeing. It was like someone trying to describe an apple to a person who has never tasted one before. You can use all of the adjectives you want, but there is nothing you can really say to express the taste of biting into the crisp skin of a fresh picked fruit and experiencing the explosion of sweet-tartness when you crunch on the refreshing flesh of the tender meat inside. I thought I'd give it a shot. As my eyes scanned the millions of twinkling lights smiling at me from above, I was amused by the thought that someone looking into all this vastness could possibly think that they could define what I was seeing. Do those guys with the million dollar telescopes really expect me to believe that they can name every star, or even begin to explain what's going on up there? If there was ever a case to be made for God or His unfathomably huge presence, looking into the sky on a clear summer night would certainly do the trick (Romans 1:19,20). I felt like a speck of sand. A very chilly, under-dressed, over-tired, speck of sand.
    I have always prided myself on being one of those forward-thinking people who embrace the gray areas of the faith. More than once I've found myself looking down my nose at those who are imprisoned by their legalism and traditionalism. Parading around as a

free-man-in-Christ has been a banner that I've displayed with honor. Recently however, I'm wondering if a little good old black and white in my diet might be a welcome relief. I still believe that God is too big to be defined by man's puny attempts. I maintain that putting God in a doctrinal box is like trying to contain an atomic blast in a pill bottle. What's starting to get on my nerves is all the mystery memos that seem to be coming from the Home Office. I can appreciate that He sees a million different angles when I can only grasp my perspective, and maybe one or two others, but some clear directive would be really helpful every now and then. Can't He just cut me a break being that, unlike Him, I am so very time-challenged? Does everything really have to be so complicated? When life is coming at me like chocolates on an I Love Lucy assembly line, how do I maintain my sanity? Should I take up a collection to get God a text-messaging plan, or is there a way to extract some black and white from all of the avalanches of gray?

The night before Jesus' final visit to Jerusalem, He very mater-of-factly told his disciples to go ahead of Him and borrow a donkey that would be found tied to a specific post in a specific place. The narrative here is extremely brief. You almost get the impression that the Apostles were becoming a little jaded to Jesus' phenomenal powers by this point. They didn't even balk or question. And sure enough, the mule was exactly where He said it would be. Compared to everything else supernatural that was going on, the whole event was pretty tame. Feeling as buried as I do recently by so many unexpected twists and turns in the path of my life, I started thinking about that ass. About it's owners. About what led up to it being tied to that post that evening. The animal's presence at that specific place and time was the result of probably nothing overly spectacular. It's owners were just going about their normal days' affairs, completely unaware that their very common, everyday decisions leading up to that night would provide a notoriety to their pet like none other. I read no reason to believe that the donkey's owners tied him up every night, hoping and waiting for the Messiah to show up and draft him into history. In fact, I'd bet that they had plans for that donkey to suit their own purposes. Everything that happened in the life of that unsuspecting animal led up to Jesus' Triumphal Entry, unbeknownst to anyone but God Himself.

I've been asking God "Why?" a lot recently. There seem to be a million different puzzle pieces, completely unrelated to one another, cropping up in my life on a daily basis. Important pieces, but confusingly disjointed from the direction that I thought my life was taking. I'm not a puzzle person. I'm way too impatient. As far as I'm concerned the phrase "to be continued" should be outlawed. During one of my unfortunate prison stays, I ran in to a practice that fascinated me. In the dayroom of the block on which I was living were five tables for people to sit at to play cards, or chess, to doodle or to write. Mostly, they were a hot commodity and dominated by guys loudly and passionately playing Spades. On one of the tables however, there was always a jigsaw puzzle in the works. Throughout the day, one or more of the residents would stop by to work on the puzzle, maybe have a cup of coffee and brief conversation with the other visiting puzzlers, and then move on. At one point or another just about everyone would take part in piecing the tiny cardboard cut-outs together. The final piece insertion was no big deal, and the completed canvas was never left on the table more than a couple of hours before it was broken apart and a new puzzle started. If I were in charge of the puzzle, my motivation would have been completing the picture on the box, and getting it done as quickly as possible, but the guys on J-Block seemed to be inspired by a higher goal. The puzzle to me, was a puzzle itself. If I had placed the last piece, you can be darn sure I would have made sure it stayed intact, and maybe hung on a wall for everyone to see. You would be amazed what you can do with toothpaste and toilet paper.

I'm starting to think that maybe God is the ultimate puzzler. Jesus' donkey was just a single piece of the puzzle that night, expertly placed and vitally important to the final picture, but in and of itself no more noticeably crucial than any of the other thousands of pieces that led

Jesus to the Cross at that appointed time in history. As I read the Word, I can see God holding a tiny puzzle piece in His hand, contemplating its placement and staring down at His work-in-progress. I can see His puzzle-placement expertise when I read in Job how intimately acquainted He is with all the finite workings of our world (Job 38-41), or when I'm told that every hair on my head is counted, or that every one of my days is written in His book before one of them comes to be (Psalm 139:13-16). All of the things in my life that are making my head spin, and my faith waver are maybe, just parts of a puzzle that I can't see a home for yet. We don't get too many bright-light-from-heaven miracles nowadays. Mostly, God's interventions are subtle, almost unnoticeable orchestrations of events and situations that become obvious only when seen in the light of specific circumstances. Perhaps every "why?" I've been pummeling at Him is one more piece of the puzzle of a design that I'm not supposed to see. Yet.

It's so easy for me to be a man of faith when all the pieces fit together. I love to challenge the puzzlers who have graduated no further than fitting round pieces into round holes and square pieces into square holes. But I have to wonder, am I really willing to throw away the goal of the finished product and find joy in allowing God to fit piece by piece together until one day the final picture is revealed? Do I trust Him that much? Perhaps it's time to realize that my life in Christ isn't the tableaux of grays I so pridefully find comfort in, but in fact a whole spectrum of colors, some that can't even be found in a box of *Crayolas*®. Colors that humble me to my knees. Shades of life that bring glory to God and replace my impertinent "why?" with gratitude and awe. God deserves so much more than I can possibly give. Often more than I am willing to give. Thank you Lord for the pieces of the puzzle that don't seem to fit. One day, they will, and when they do, I will see clearly, even as I am so very clearly and intimately seen, by You (1 Corinthians 13:12).

A Gaping Hole

I am broken. I don't mean the kind of broken you become when you are humbled to your knees and brought to tears by weakness or heart brokenness. I mean the kind of broken like a yo-yo without a string. I don't work right. There is just some part of my brain that doesn't process things correctly. When I am overwhelmed I want to reach for drugs. When I am hurt, I want to hurt back. When I am feeling my weakest or most vulnerable, I would rather wallow in my own self-pity than try to make things better. Or reach out to the One who can.

Logically, I understand and believe to the core of my being that all humans are broken. It's the result of man's fall in the Garden of Eden. I struggle along day by day fighting this war that exists inside of me. It's a terrible battle. Donald Miller, in his book, *Searching For God Knows What*[1] describes the fall of man tantamount to the desecration of Chernobyl. When Adam and Eve decided to break their connection with God, a chain of events was initiated that has multiplied millions of times over to the point that what was once God's playground has now become His battleground. Misery and ugliness are rampant. The society in which we live doesn't look anything at all like that which God intended. Things are a mess. No matter how many dollars we throw at the problem it will still be ten times worse tomorrow. Everything around us is dying and no matter how hard we try, it can't be fixed. Adam and Eve's simple act of defiance not only broke us, but broke God's heart into a million pieces.

When I even try to imagine the devastation it gives me chills. The love that God had for His first creations was literally thrown back in

His face. And we are still doing it today. I know I am. Imagine what it must have been like in the Garden of Eden, walking with God hand in hand, never questioning for one minute that His love and generosity was the source of life. How must God have felt when his children hid from Him? So incredulous was He, that His first words to fallen man were not a rebuke, but to question the reality of the situation, "Who told you that you were naked?" Imagine your wife or husband of fifty years waking up one morning and saying. "I don't love you anymore." Like an atomic blast.

Trying to understand the ramifications and the extent to which God subjected Himself to heal the rift is catastrophically mind-numbing as well. I don't think **anyone** can really grasp the weight of it all. Before the fall, man was whole. Nowadays we are all running around trying to find our completeness by trying to be the most popular, the richest, and the best. We find our satisfaction in superiority. We find our sense of well-being by associating with beliefs or standards of whatever makes us feel the strongest or most acceptable. We seek affirmation wherever we can find it. We'll do anything and everything we can to fill the hole that Adam and Eve's disobedience left inside of us. Like refugees of a nuclear holocaust we spend our lives trying to find the one thing that was lost in the Garden: a relationship with our Creator. God's love.

Jesus didn't seem to have this problem though. It's probably why He was considered an outcast and a heretic. He had no need to be the best, the richest or the most powerful. He was whole, content and secure in who He was, God's child. He felt most comfortable with society's outcasts, the people who couldn't play the better-than-you game. He spoke truth without reservation because He knew the source of His life was God. The tears He cried were not over losing the competition, they were over the ravages of sin to His dearly loved world. Ironically, the folks with whom Jesus did run into a problem were those who claimed to have it all together, religiously speaking. Jesus lived the Edenic reality amidst refugees of the fall. It must break

God's heart that so many religious organizations would kick Jesus out on His keester if He showed up at a church service today. He would upset the cart and unbalance the hierarchy. Probably He wouldn't show up to one committee meeting because He was busy at the local AIDS clinic or was out comforting some strung-out addict on the streets. I wonder how God feels about the fact that gay men and woman have their own churches because they are not accepted by mainline Christianity? Jesus was a radical because He lived without that gaping hole in His soul that we all struggle with everyday in this very broken, infected world.

I am saved only because God is so loving and generous that He has provided me a life outside of the black hole. Or, more succinctly, He filled it with Himself. It has nothing to do with anything I did or could ever do. I'm broken. This body I live in doesn't know any better than to seek solace in whatever I can put my hands on to feel right, or at least acceptable. I always want to think of me first. When I take a good hard look at who I am, and who I should and want to be, the idea that I am a sinner is no problem for me to accept. In fact, it's a no-brainer. What I find really difficult to swallow is that God wants me to be fulfilled by His love, and that because of His unfathomable grace, He is there to help me with every step along the journey. That's the brain-buster.

Though some intellectuals and theologians may disagree, I really believe that sin is more than just a specific act. It is a state of mind. James says that, "Anyone, then, who knows the good he ought to do and doesn't do it, sins." (4:17), and Paul goes to great lengths to explain that everything is permissible, but not necessarily beneficial (Romans 14; 1 Corinthians 10:23-34). It is the mindset that I am god that gets me in to trouble. Rules and checklists "have an appearance of godliness…, but they lack any value in restraining sensual indulgence." (Colossians 2:23). What got broken that day that Adam and Eve ate the fruit was a relationship. A relationship that is the source of life and completeness. And it's only when I nurture my newly rescued relationship with my Creator that I can even hope to stop looking at the world's answers of success and wholeness and peace, and begin to find the love that is the true foundation of my life.

It's a vicious battle. It's so much easier to pop a pill, eat a box of Oreos®, purchase some contentment or just identify myself with societies' winners. I seem to spend more time fighting than living, and my definition of living too easily finds itself in that which I know it shouldn't. I'm broken because I am human. I spend my life seeking acceptance and success. I don't ever feel loved enough. It's no wonder that Jesus put so much emphasis on offering a new kind of rest from life's burdens and accusations. "Come to me, all you who are weary and burdened, and I will give you rest" (Matthew 11:28). "Peace I leave with you; my peace I give you. I do not give to you as the world gives. Do not let your hearts be troubled and do not be afraid." (John 14:27). How much different would my life be if I understood that more than help through difficulties and struggles, Jesus is offering His source of life as my source of life? If I could just get it through my thick head that He is all I need, maybe I could spend more time helping others than seeking help myself, giving more than needing, loving more than seeking to be loved. Maybe, just maybe, all the failures and mistakes in my life are not so much because I am a snot-faced, disobedient child of God but because I am a broken refugee of the fall, and everything that I so desperately need and long for is right in front of my face. If I would just allow God to be the source of my existence. I am so grateful that God is so diligently persistent at trying to drive this fact home to me. Maybe, one day, I'll even listen. I hope that one day I can look in the mirror and see myself as the Apostle John saw himself as "the one Jesus loves."

Tough Cookie Training

Often, when people hear that I spent time in prison they want to know if it's anything like what you see in the movies. Really, it's not. The basics are there, hard cement floors, metal bars, egotistical corrections officers, but the reality is far from anything I have ever seen accurately portrayed. I don't think that there is a way to capture on film the ever-present feeling of unrest born from endless hours of boredom, or the impending violence that can erupt without even a moment's warning. Air that is permeated by desperation of hundreds, sometimes thousands of men feeling lost lonely, unforgiven and forgotten in a system that is, in reality, designed to pad the wallets of lawyers and politicians while perceived by the general public as a place for correction and rehabilitation. Years upon years of grade X food, waiting for mail that never arrives and unending noise create a feeling of constant angst and apprehension far worse than Hollywood's dramatized visions of rape and gang dominance that hardly exist, because the participants are willing and relations are governed by racial cliques. The majority of the population feel wrongly convicted and victimized. Anger and frustration are a way of life.

The one thing that always struck me about being a member of this warehoused society is that it doesn't take long to realize that the people around you are just that, people; individuals with families, personalities, talents. You don't run across the forensically insane. You shower and eat with fathers, brothers, sons, business men, artists, athletes, Christians, etc. All who have one thing in common. They got caught. The honest correctional officer will tell you that that's the only difference between those in uniform and those in stripes. I celled with a guy for almost nine months who was probably one of the most positively influential men I have ever had the privilege of knowing. When I would start letting my guard down, something you can never afford to do, he would pull me aside and quietly say, "Adam, you're getting loose." It was his way of reminding me that I could never indulge in the luxury of getting too comfortable where I was. His words have been ringing in my ears lately. I've been getting loose.

In the eleventh chapter of Hebrews, there are men and women, listed by name, that the writer commends for their faith. All the bigwigs are present and accounted for, Enoch, Noah, Elijah, Abraham, David, etc. Each one introduced and qualified by their acts of faith. It's quite an impressive roll-call. A hall of fame, if you will. Having read this chapter so many times over the years, I have to admit that I sometimes skim through the stories because they are so familiar to me. However, no matter how lazy I am with the details there is one phrase that never fails to grab my attention, partly because it has been repeatedly highlighted and underlined with such enthusiasm that the paper is practically transparent. "All these people were still living by faith when they died. They did not receive the things promised; they only saw them and welcomed them from a distance. And they admitted that they were **aliens and strangers on earth**." (verse 13). These were men and women who for the most part, could proudly claim citizenship as Israelites, yet lived as foreigners in a foreign land. A way of life very reminiscent of Jesus' admonishment, "where your treasure is, there your heart will be also" (Matthew 6:21). It seems that possession of a spiritual green card is a theme that runs through most of the New Testament. The Apostle Paul puts it this way, "So we fix our eyes not on what is seen, but on what is unseen. For what is seen is temporary, but what is unseen is eternal." (2 Corinthians 4:18). Heavenly citizenship is obviously a state of the heart, not the mind. It's a life-encompassing perspective that simply can't be achieved by following rules or lists of do's and don't's. To be quite honest, I sometimes prefer the rules. When Jesus said that the kingdom of God is at hand, it's no wonder he confused the religious zealots of His day. They were looking for something that they could see with their eyes and reason with their minds. Jesus was trying to tell them that it is our citizenship that defines the reality of faith, not who we know, what we do or where we go. The fragrance of our lives comes from a perspective that is anchored in the presence of God.

I love the story of Jonah. Not because it's sort of cool to think of surfing the waves inside of a giant fish, but because I am so much like him in so many ways. I've ridden those waves. He often gets a bad rap, but really he is just a regular guy struggling with the focus of his own heavenly perspective, being human and all. First of all, he couldn't have been such a bad fella if God chose and entrusted him with the responsibility of bringing a message of salvation to a whole nation, a people that He valued enough to warn and offer a second chance. Jonah must have had something going in his favor in God's eyes. Yet after coming face to face with his Creator, (I don't know if he was scared, or just felt unworthy), Jonah immediately decides to hop the next boat out of town. He actually thinks that he can hide from God's purpose for him. Definitely been there and done that. I might sound all spiritual and introspective about my years behind bars, but really, to this day, even the sound of a passing police siren makes my stomach tighten and my skin crawl. It doesn't take long inside the fishes gut for Jonah to realize that slopping around in bile and entrails is God's not so subtle way of telling him to get a grip, and he starts singing some pretty poetry pretty quick. A song of gratitude I believe it was. Vomited up on the shore, Jonah wastes no time trying to fix what he messed up in the first place. He has a job to do. Maybe still a little woozy from his intestinal cruise, he approaches his mission with visions of grandeur. He assumed that he would be calling down fire and brimstone on a whole country. Jonah was probably bragging to all of his friends over a night's pint of ale, "Oh yeah, I'm the man!" So when the Ninevites repent, Jonah feels lost and forgotten. He gets downright depressed. I could be looking in a mirror. God doesn't for one second give up. By the end of the story, Ninevah is saved, and so is Jonah.

I had a really rough night at work tonight. The restaurant was crazy busy and it seemed like the kitchen ran out of everything just before my table ordered it. I had a family leave me a fifty cent tip because they thought that their food took too long, even though I kept assuring them that you just can't rush a well-done steak. As I was closing out their check, angry and frustrated, wishing I could find these people in the parking lot and fling the two quarters at their heads, another server started to brag about how he was, "burning up the floor, making tips out the wazoo, turning and burning and ready for his next victims." His self-back patting was so absurd that I started to feel sorry for him, and then for the family who stormed out full but unhappy. I let my guard down by getting angry. If my biggest victory in life is a thirty percent tip or my biggest failure is a table of guests whom I couldn't schmooze out of their choice to be miserable and rude, then my treasure is far from being stored where it should be. It all made me start thinking about a lot of the things that I've been feeling and doing lately. It's so easy to get distracted from what's really important and to start feeling sorry for myself. To try to orchestrate my own peace and destiny. To use Jesus instead of letting Him use me. Really, Jonah put himself in the belly of that fish, and a little bit of history was re-written when he got himself out. The first part of one of my personal favorite Bible verses is found in 2 Corinthians (16-18). It's a text that I like to refer to as "tough-cookie training. " It reminds me that although attitudes and circumstances may cause me to "get loose," my ever-patient Creator is always right there ready to help me to unfray my edges and reaffirm my true citizenship, in His loving arms.

As I drove home, I prayed for the impatient family, and for the other server who was so proud of his financial success. Later on, after dropping the quarters in my change jar, I asked God to forgive me for losing sight of what is really important. Then I thanked Him for His incredible generosity. I asked Him if I could have another shot at tightening things up, with His help and guidance of course. I don't want to end up back in the belly of my own institutional fish; a place where I have already spent way too much time. Then I thanked Him for that too.

Therefore we do not lose heart. Though outwardly we are wasting away, yet inwardly we are being renewed day by day. For our light and momentary troubles are achieving for us an eternal glory that far outweighs them all. So we fix our eyes not on what is seen, but on what is unseen. For what is seen is temporary, but what is unseen is eternal.
2 Corinthians 4:16-18

Sweet Dreams

I decided the other day to put up or shut up. I really like the idea that the Bible, God's Word, is more a story of God's relationship with man than a rule book. It certainly helps me to resolve all of those pesky swarming gnats of do's and don't's that some traditions like to corner me with. For me, the biggest problem with approaching His Word as a manual has always been that as hard as I try to behave, I end up living under a storm cloud of guilt, instead of the gentle breeze of faith I'm supposed to. I bet other people feel this way too. Who can blame anyone for acting skiddish around a religion that keeps score? So I opened my Bible. Not the easy-to-read Message Version, but the good old reliable New International Version. Genesis. Chapter one. Verse one.

This time, I decided not to search for hidden meaning or deeply spiritual warm-fuzzies. I opened my mind to the idea that this is a novel, like a John Grisham or Danielle Steel. Since I love to read just about anything, this approach was not something foreign to me. I simply opened the cover and trusted the author to guide me on the journey that He penned. Perhaps the time has come to show the same openness and confidence to the most prolific author of all that I would put in some Doubleday superstar. The more I re-experienced the familiar stories being played out on the pages in front of me, the more my mind began to envision a storyteller. In the back of my head, I envisioned a comfortable grandfather-figure, Grandpa Walton comes to mind, rocking in his chair on the porch swing on a breezy summer night telling me stories about the good old days.

I'll admit, the book of Genesis has always sort of bothered me. There are way too many seeming inconsistencies. Did Cain and Abel marry their sisters, or cousins? Where did all the people in the story of the Tower of Babel come from? And that's just to name two. As I explored the possible explanations in my head, pieces of the puzzle began to fall in to place. If, the Bible is the yarn of some unfathomably enormous Being, what's to say that what we are reading isn't only one of many stories that the Creator could tell. The difference is that this is the central story, around which all other stories revolve. It is the preface and the epilogue. I also realized a funny thing about the English word, "man". It can indicate either singular or plural. We read that God created man, are there perhaps other miraculous examples of God's involvement whose stories have gone untold? God still involved. Redemption still found through Jesus. Each story a precious gem, reflecting the light of God's ginormous love. Each a beloved chronicle cherished in the heart of the Almighty. Lot's and lot's of stories.

When you scratch a mosquito bite until it bleeds, you don't keep clawing away because you want to break the skin. You scratch because it feels good. After each creation, in the book of Genesis, the writer tells us that God was pleased with what He had accomplished. You would think though, that when He created Adam, he wouldn't have allowed for the possibility of treachery or disobedience. He should have been the forever perfect and obedient man. If there is one lesson, I never fail to walk away with after reading The Bible is that creating man, without free-will, would have completely defeated God's purpose for creation at all. There are a million different facets of love, but perhaps, one of the most brilliant is that it is only genuine if freely chosen. You can't make someone love you, no matter how hard you try. Love always comes from the heart, and although functionally, science may have developed a synthetic version, not even the greatest minds in the world can recreate love without willing participation of the participant. Though love may be a slippery emotion, it is the state of the heart upon which God created towering mountains and crashing seas. Love is not genuine unless it is a personal choice.[2]

A YEAR FOR DAD

With this new mindset, I discovered some amazing things. All those holes in the Bible's first book that always left me scratching my head, are not really missing puzzle pieces at all. They are just footnotes to the primary story that's being told. The Author's theme is God's love for man; anything that has to do with that storyline is included, anything unnecessary is left out. Our Father in Heaven, the consummate editor, provides exactly and specifically only that which leads us to Jesus' cross on Golgatha. What might at first glance seem to be question marks are actually exclamation points. Even in the smallest ways, the story of God's love for His children holds the spotlight fast.

Even in the minute details, we are treated with only information that includes God's involvement. Taking this approach, it seems that God interjects anything that has to do with His participation in the story, even at the risk of creating mental detours. What really brought this idea to light was a fella I ran across who is mentioned only briefly in the narrative of Joseph's life. I've never heard a sermon preached about him, I don't believe that he is ever mentioned again in Scripture, but he was a living, breathing person, with a story of his own, whom God used to direct His child's path. Joseph was sent by his father to go look for his brothers while they tended the flocks. The Bible says that Jacob's boy was wandering around and around until a man found him and told him precisely where they would be. That's it. Pretty much, two lines and he is done. His importance however is incalculable. He directed Joseph to his brothers, who in turn sold him to the passing Gypsies, which began a chain of events that would see him ruling over all of Egypt, and, eventually, rescuing and reuniting his entire clan. I wonder if the man who gave Joseph directions even had a second thought about the young boy whom he had found wandering in the fields that day (Genesis 37:14-18). Did he mention it to his wife over dinner, or tell his children so as to warn them not to be wanderers themselves? I thought a lot about this guy. He was both essential and inconsequential, yet God used him so powerfully. I realized that his purpose was to bring glory to God and remain in anonymity. Then I thought about Melchizedek the mystery Priest, and Simeon who carried Jesus' cross for Him, and Nicodemus, and Gamaliel, the Pharisee, who publicly acknowledged the possibility that Jesus was actually who He claimed to be. We know their names, but we know so little of their stories. What we do know about all of them, and many more, is that they represent a point in history, that God stepped in to time and expressed His love for man in a very specific way, with a very specific purpose.

So Joseph buries his Dad, and his brothers start to think, "Uh-oh, the old man's gone. This guy could turn on us, fast." I picture Joseph, who is no longer the gangly adolescent at his brothers' mercy. He has run one of the greatest empires known to man. The wrinkles around his eyes and mouth tell the tale of his years wrongly imprisoned, and the sleepless nights he must have spent thinking about his Dad and brothers. In response to their fear, the words slip out of his mouth as if to mock the absurdity of this concept. He wouldn't have it any other way. "You intended to harm me, but God intended it for good to accomplish what is now being done, the saving of many lives." (Gen. 50:20) Story after story. That's what The Book is all about.

The Bible is the perfect guidebook for those of us who live in the Age of Faith. Though culturally, we couldn't be more different than the societies portrayed, God is still as intricately involved today as He ever was. It would be nice if the Trinity could get together and do an updated version, but then, it wouldn't be about faith would it? Guess God had to put down His pen and publish at some point. I think it's really interesting that we are left with this sort of cultural museum. Reading about the different customs and how God worked within the structure of that society helps me to understand how contemporary God is to me. He's internet savvy and goes to 12 step meetings. Probably, He even watches "Father Knows Best" reruns. Wouldn't it be awesome to hear one of Jesus' messages in 21st Century vernacular?

I like the idea that reading His Word is like curling up on my Heavenly Father's lap and being told stories. Stories of His mercy, and grace and kindness. It's a very comforting place to be. I just can't help but to walk away knowing more about the God who created me. And through the intimacy of His narrative, I can't help but experience the transforming of His indwelling Spirit when His words touch my heart or cut through my soul. Like a child who rests in the safety of his Daddy's unconditionally loving arms, I find myself cooing for more tales of God's faithfulness, generosity and creativity as the central character of all the stories that He tells. No guilt. No condemnation. Just all-encompassing love. Living, active, sharper than a double-edged sword. Sometimes as one of my crazy days at work is beginning to come to an end, I plan my dinner in my head and enjoy the thought of curling up with God. His Word wraps itself around my spirit and my mind reminding me, that even when it is storming rain outside, I am warm and cozy resting in His everlasting arms.

An Angel Named Gabe

My daughter is all grown up now. My regular joke is that, "my kids are 20-this and 20-that. They're just not so cute at that age." Humor helps you to get better tips. I'm pretty much experiencing the age-appropriate, "my kids never call me enough" syndrome. Truth is it stinks. I liked it a whole lot better when she was little, and needed me. Even adored me. It was a pretty heady experience. I like that they've grown-up, I even like them as grown-ups. Unfortunately, peppering my paternal reverie, is the knowledge that I royally messed things up, and they now carry unnecessary and unfair baggage with them wherever they go. Just like I do from the unwitting mistakes of my parents. Life would be so much easier with a permanent bellboy on staff to carry everything for you.

My little peanut is married too. She's doing an awesome job of it. I used to say that my daughter was me, without the baggage. I still see the best of me in her. I also see some of her mom in her. Her Mom is an organizer and a methodically careful person. I'm more Peter Pan. The ex is the spiritual traditionalist. I am the bohemian ragamuffin. I appreciate her commitment and tenacity. She wonders if I'm actually saved. I keep trying to love her and live in forgiveness. She would rather just forget that I even exist. I attempted once to cross the boundary of intimacy with her at my daughter's wedding and all she could respond was, "I can't." I really wonder what that means. Honestly, with all the water under the bridge, she remains one of the most positively influential people in my life, and I am grateful to have had the privilege of spending over a decade with her.

In the book of Hebrews it says that we should be nice to people because we could be entertaining angels. I don't really think about angels a lot. I believe that they are here helping us (Hebrews 1:14). I like Frank Peretti's description of an invisible spiritual world happening in and around us, in his book This Present Darkness.[3] For some reason, whenever I read that verse about entertaining angels, I got the impression that these humanoid angels touched your life and then just disappeared. It doesn't really say that. Maybe we do each have a guardian angel and he is so intimately associated with us, in the realm we cannot see, that people in our lives, regular players, could be the angels referred to here. My son-in-law's name is Gabriel.

I have to admit, there are times I like him better than my biological son or daughter. He's so normal, and kind, and generous. So my daughter, who has not yet fully recovered from the sins of my past, goes and marries this stable, rational guy. God is such a hoot. Gabe has a great family, who love Jesus. Maybe all those years behind bars praying for her really paid off. I see bits of me in him too. The good stuff. It's awesome. He keeps in touch. He lets me know what's going on. He's even one told off the ex-wife. I love this guy! Couldn't be happier. Sounds like angel material to me.

Embedded in the early Apple Macintosh® operating systems were these things called Easter Eggs. Basically, if you ran across one, you clicked on it and it would be something just to make you smile, a picture, a joke. I'm starting to think that life is full of these Easter Eggs that you just stumble across. Their sole intention is to make you smile. I can't even begin to understand why God takes such pleasure in us. But He does. From sunsets, to kittens and chocolate there are Easter eggs all over the place. It's sort of like being a Mario Brother. A few years ago, Oprah suggested that her audience close every day with five things they are thankful for that day. I did it for over a year. I don't know why I stopped. I need to start again. Instead of sweating life's inevitable potholes, it just makes sense to focus on the positive. It's there, you just have to look for it a little harder some times than others. Trusting God does it for me. I like to pray, "I can't wait to see how You work this one out," instead of, "this is how I want it to work out." It's the difference between an adventure and a struggle. It's not always easy. I have to admit, I've been known to read the last chapter of a novel before the first. I can be an impatient son-of-a-gun.

Whenever I go to the Hallmark® store at the mall, I'm usually in a rush to buy a birthday card that I should have sent out several days before. As I am making a bee-line to the line of 99-centers, I never cease to notice collections of little statuettes of angels displayed all over the place. Some of them have the adorable faces of cherubic children in endearing poses and positions. Others look like the monuments you would see in the garden of someone who has pink flamingos on their front lawn. Others are wearing costumes of varied professions and hobbyists: doctors, layers, teachers, golfers, tennis players and usually an overwhelmed mother or two. I've noticed that angels even have their own decorating motifs, from bedspreads to bathroom trash cans. They have become quite an industry.

There is really not a lot of mention of these heavenly beings in the Bible. Isaiah tells us that Lucifer is a fallen angel. The prophet Ezekiel describes them as having eyes all over their heads and a lot of wings that flap around like flags in a tornado. As I mentioned before, the writer of the book of Hebrews tells us that angels exist as ministering spirits sent to serve those who will inherit salvation. Mythologists love them, and apparently greeting card companies do too. I just don't give them a lot of thought. I don't think a lot about gravity or how airplanes stay in the air either. I don't feel obliged to have all the answers. Frankly, I think questions are a whole lot more fun. What I do know for certain is that God can do or use anything to reach into history and accomplish His purposes. I have experienced it, and I count on it. Once He made a donkey talk (Numbers 22:28-30). I guess that's what faith is about. It's something that we believe to be true that doesn't have to make perfect sense (Hebrews 11:1). I don't know about you, but when I have all the answers I tend to get a little cocky and self-righteous. It's exciting to think that something special is going to happen on my birthday, or something magical will happen on

Christmas. The Easter Bunny is kind of cool too, though I'm not clear on the connection between rabbits and colored eggs. What would life be without the sense of wonder, or awe. Or faith.

I have never actually seen an angel, that I know of. When Gabe came in to my daughter's life, I breathed a sigh of relief. Doesn't every Dad want a guardian angel for his child? If the Bible says angels exist, then they do; obviously it's a subject that's on a need-to-know basis of spiritual matters. What I am certain of is that God takes great pleasure in watching over us, and making our hearts smile. Today's tragedies can be either just that, or opportunities for God to be God. There are no hollow mushy malted milk balls in God's box of Whoppers®. So, if I have spiritual company following me as it says in the book of Hebrews, there is one more thing I know for sure. There's a very patient angel somewhere with a great sense of humor!

God Knows

    I have to admit, except for his followers' penchant for leaving Bible's in hotel rooms, I've never really paid a whole lot of attention to Gideon either. He is one of those Old Testament guys whose name everyone knows, but whose story seems to be overshadowed by stiff paged volumes in the back of every Howard Johnsons® dresser drawer. I'm glad that they're there. I'm sure that someone must read them. But why has God seen fit to make sure that anyone who has ever been in a hotel room knows his name? Maybe this is one of those question marks that God wants to turn into an exclamation point.
    I've been in love exactly twice in my life. It didn't work out too well either time, but while I was ankle deep, it was like nothing I could have ever imagined. The honeymoon period of love is rolling in a vat of chocolate. There is some kind of cosmic connection with the other person that you feel when you fall in love. God describes the intimacy between two people who have permanently committed their lives to each other as becoming one. Really, it's a great description. The other person becomes all you can think about, everything you do is motivated by wanting to experience more of them; waged and crimes committed. Being head over heals in love is like walking on a floor covered by marbles, and the confounding part about it is that even when you fall flat on your butt, you get up and try to walk again.
    In over twenty-five years of being a Christian, I've never been able to really wrap my brain around the fact that God loves me that much. Sure, God so loved the world, but me? He loves me that much? Maybe it's a case of love being blind, because certainly, someone as phenomenal as our Creator must just be clumping me into the whole.

It's got to be like when you buy those assorted mini-boxes of cereal. Most of them are delicious, but there is always one in there that ends up in the back of the cabinet, uneaten and forgotten. You still buy the assortment and just accept the fact that one of the eight containers is something that you will never eat. If He knows me as well as He says He does, I can't fathom that I'm the reason He's buying the whole package. Whenever someone says to me, "Jesus loves you," I'm thinking cereal.

We can pretty much assume, on an intellectual basis, that God is not only intimately acquainted with all our way but that He also adores every single one of His creations. There are a bunch of Scriptures that teach this fact. Gideon's place in history is not an accident. It was very purposed in fact, just like yours and mine. Picture it, a harsh desert, a restless tribe. God sends a leader, blows away any question that He is who He claims to be. The leader dies. The nation starts worshipping beetles and bovine. Over and over. Finally, Gideon is up at bat. God says to him, "The Lord is with you, mighty warrior." Gideon responds, "If the Lord is with us, why has all this happened to us?" God sighs. The whole interaction is really kind of funny. When God finally has him just about convinced that he's supposed to be the man of the hour, Gideon begins to shuffle,. "how can I save Israel? My clan is the weakest in Manasseh, and I am the least in my family." Then just to add icing on the cake, Gideon basically says, "ok God, look, I'll do what you want me to do, just pass one little test for me." When God is finally done jumping through Gideon's hoops, Gideon shrinks back like a schoolgirl and says, "Ah ["AHH!" My words], Sovereign Lord! I have seen the angel of the Lord face to face!" This stuff burning my finger really IS fire.

Does, Gideon begin to glow in the dark now that he understands who He is dealing with? Maybe on the outside. He does what God wants him to do, but at night, so his family won't catch him. When the sun comes up, so does his mask as he proclaims, "If Baal really is god, he can defend himself when someone breaks down his altar." He is so convincing that they even give him a cool nickname to commemorate his heroism. He had everyone fooled. Not God.

If you keep reading Gideon's story, Judges chapters 6-8, there is so much more. Gideon never completely stopped being Gideon. If God Almighty shares my sense of sardonic humor, and I think He may, then He may have been doing a little more than providing us an object lesson when he slowly, and methodically whittled down Gideon's army to a mere 300 men. I suspect that God does like to play sometimes, but never without a purpose, and it's always maddeningly personal. As Gideon must have been starting to hyper-ventilate over the size of what was left of his troops, his loving Heavenly father throws him a paper bag, and says, "it's ok, breathe. If you are afraid of what's going to happen, go on down and listen to their plans, and you will be comforted when you see how easily this battle will be won" (7:10-15). God knew everything there was to know about Gideon. God loved Gideon. God believed in Gideon. God used Gideon. So profound was the effect of Gideon's life that he is the one Judge who's absence is specifically attributed to Israel's moral decline at the time.

Gideon is me. I can talk a good talk, but in the most intimate places of my life, that only God and myself are privy to, I doubt, I test, and I sin. Then, without even batting an eye, He helps me up, He wipes me off and sets me on my way. Everytime. I've come to the point in my life that when I do fall, and repent, I no longer think that God is mad at me and has to get over it. I think that I hurt His heart when I disobey. If Jesus wept over the untimely loss of his friend because of the ravages of sin (John 11:1-44), certainly He's cried a million tears over me.

Have you ever had that dream when you are trying to scream for help and nothing will come out of your mouth? God must feel like that a lot. This incredible story of how much God knows us and still loves and uses us is screaming from a dresser drawer in every hotel room around the world. I'm sure that many people have been blessed by having a Bible available in a time of need, or even boredom. I think it's cool that God, knowing in detail every person that would ever open a drawer containing a Bible placed by the Gideon Society® left an arrow pointing directly to Him. I would imagine too that over the years, people have responded differently to seeing the Book unexpectedly lying right there in front of them. Some reactions were probably not so favorable. All good to God. They couldn't help conjuring the name. And I can't help walking away from the account of Gideon's life without being convinced, just a little bit more, that even though I'm still me, He has a place in His kingdom and His heart, just for me.

Love is Like That

    I hate to wait. I don't mind so much if there is something to do to keep me busy while I'm waiting, but to just linger makes me crazier than I already am. It's the reason I'm a much better cook than I am a baker. When you cook there's usually something to stir, or prepare, or at least some mess to clean up. Baking requires sticking something in the oven, closing the door, and setting a timer. The reason I don't wear a wristwatch is because it makes me too aware of the slowness of seconds ticking away when I have nothing better to do than stare at it's mocking face. I'm also the last person you would want to go shopping with. I prefer the self-checkout at the grocery store because staring at headlines on Reader's Digest© and the National Inquirer© do nothing to quell the growing urge in me to just run screaming out the electronic doors. Come to think of it, half the time, they don't even open up fast enough. God does have his hands full with me.
    When I was a preacher, I used to joke that God was from the South because He moves so slowly. Have you ever noticed that? Immediate answers to prayer come few and far between. There's usually a preparation, or a process or a preface, or a *pr-something*. Computer geeks have an axiom similar to Murphy's Law called McCutcheon's Law. It goes, "Before you can do anything, you have to do something else first." As a person who does some website design, I can assure you that it is completely true. It also seems that spiritual matters are subject to the same principle. The problem I find is that often, the something you have to do first is a big old question mark. Yesterday, I discovered the answer to a question mark that I've been struggling with for quite a while now, and I didn't like it. Not one bit.

There is an old hymn that exclaims, "you will know we are Christians by our love." It is often followed more the modern praise song, "love, love, love, love, the Gospel in a word is love." Love is clearly the theme of God's Word. God's love for man. It is what draws us to the cross in the first place. It is what steadies our feet when we are stumbling. It is the very essence of who God is (1 John 4:16). Needless to say, pages and pages could be written on the subject. Paul's definition in 1 Corinthians 13 is pretty darned clear. I would say that the simplest way for me to boil it down in my brain is to understand that love is the antitheses of selfishness. Jesus lived the ideal, and we are asked by God to strive for the same. When my words, actions and motives have nothing in them for me, and everything in them for you, I am practicing the art of love. The word itself is really a synonym for holiness and religion. God intends, selflessness is to be the core motive of everything I do. It makes me wonder, in the practical workings of my life, does love define me or do I define love?

While I was at the lake again the other day, thinking these deep spiritual thoughts, a loud commotion burst right in front of me. There were some teenagers in the water making doughnuts and figure eights with their jet ski pretty close to the shore. It was a bit distracting, but my mind had already drifted off to being jealous that they had a jetski and I didn't, so I wasn't paying all that much attention. No more than five minutes into the kid's carefree maneuvers, a woman charged from out of nowhere to the group of Mom's who were enjoying the reverie by proxy. With a shrill, almost shrew-like voice, the Moms were, in no uncertain terms, informed that what their children were doing was highly illegal and that their kids should know this IF they were in fact licensed to operate the vehicle as they should be. I'm not sure if it was the heat of the day, the instinctive defensiveness of a mother whose child is being threatened or just the tone of the woman's voice, but a scuttle erupted, and I completely forgot to finish my whining to God about how much I wished I had a jetski. What the woman was saying to the Moms was right. Such speeds, so close to nearby swimmers, was potentially dangerous. She was probably even right that the law stated that a wake was not to be created any closer than a hundred feet from shore. But in my head I sided with the mothers. I didn't like that lady. She was rude and a big old spoiled sport.

I started to wonder why she would want to rain on everyone's parade like she did. What was she so angry about? Could it be a case of diplomatic school dropout? If she was really concerned for the safety of the kids and the swimmers, wouldn't she have approached the situation with a little less venom and a whole lot more loving concern? What was her motive for causing such a dramatic scene? Once the lady with the strong opinions had stormed off, threatening to notify the authorities, I started thinking about motives. Mine in particular. How much of what I say and do is actually inspired by love and how much actually carry what some would call ulterior motives. Am I acting in love by being pleasant to people, or do I just want them to like me? Do I do kind and generous things to gain acceptance? It was a pretty unsettling inventory, but I rallied. I tried to make excuses. I even fabricated a few really good rationalizations. The Holy Spirit would have none of it.

I guess that maybe while I'm waiting around for God to answer my prayers, there is something I can be doing to pass the time. In fact, I'm starting to think that maybe the delayed answers I'm looking for aren't God's fault at all. Maybe they're mine. Looking for a door to open, or even a miracle to happen doesn't require setting a timer and waiting. It's a call to action.

So let God work his will in you. Yell a loud no to the Devil and watch him scamper. Say a quiet yes to God and he'll be there in no time. Quit dabbling in sin. Purify your inner life. Quit playing the field. Hit bottom, and cry your eyes out. The fun and games are over. Get serious, really serious. Get down on your knees before the Master; it's the only way you'll get on your feet... Take

the old prophets as your mentors. They put up with anything, went through everything, and never once quit, all the time honoring God. What a gift life is to those who stay the course! You've heard, of course, of Job's staying power, and you know how God brought it all together for him at the end. That's because God cares, cares right down to the last detail...
(James 4:7-10; 5:10-11 / THE MESSAGE)

I think that God holds the answer to every one of my prayers in His hands, but He won't pass them along until I'm ready to receive them. You may or may not be aware that waiters are paid part-time summer help wages. Less than three bucks an hour. Your tip is their rent payment. I've often joked with my fellow servers that I wish people would just walk in the door, hand me my money and leave. Thinking about it in terms of the Apostles words, maybe the serving part is, in fact, more important than the tipping part. How can I expect to experience the hand of God in my life if I'm just killing time until an answer comes? It would seem that waiting on divine intervention demands a lot more responsibility than just twiddling my thumbs and distracting my impatient brain.

If love is supposed to be the motivation for everything I do, I have some real soul-searching and day-to-day work to do. All of a sudden, that prayer that I've been pleading for God to answer for so long seems like maybe it's being answered after all. Not with the resolution I've been looking for yet, but with a call to live more closely to the heart of my Heavenly Father. I realize too that the final answer may be nothing like what I'm hoping it will be, or it may be. I think that the answer I'm experiencing now will prepare me for whatever answer is to come. Being frustrated by the wait is a complete waste of time. In fact, it's only slowing down the process. It may even be a hindrance. Jesus said that I could ask Him for anything, and if I love Him, then however He chooses to answer is better than anything I could imagine or dream.

Love is like that.

God can do anything, you know—far more than you could ever imagine or guess or request in your wildest dreams! He does it not by pushing us around but by working within us, his Spirit deeply and gently within us.
(Ephesians 3:20 THE MESSAGE)

Why God, Why?

 Many years ago, I came across a pamphlet titled "Others May, You Cannot.⁴'" More than the content, the title really stuck in my head. It doesn't come up a lot, but it's a phrase that seems to jump up in my memory when I'm feeling especially jealous or resentful toward someone who has or does something I wish I could have or do. Brad Pitt and Donald Trump would be good examples. The tract was actually written in the 1800's by a fella named G.D. Watson. Googling the title will bring up several versions. The premise is that, as Christians, although there are people who get away with all kinds of behavior, and profit from it, we are each accountable to a higher standard. What is no problem for you, may be sin for me. It's really an excellent piece. Unfortunately, being the conniving manipulator of truth that I can tend to be when backed into a corner, it can also be an easy tool for self-rationalization. The phrase, "well at least I'm going to heaven" comes to mind.

 Walking in to the bowels of a prison for the first time is an indescribable feeling. It's an unfamiliar world of hatred and despair where the primary goal of each day is to wake up so you can go back to sleep. Tension fills the air like the overwhelming stench of decay and a piece of mail is more valuable than the most precious jewel. Humiliation and degradation are the daily diet. It's funny, in my present reality, I often find myself lying in bed at night re-living the experiences of those eight and half years behind the walls. The things I saw. The people I met. If you would have asked me twenty years ago if I thought I could have survived such a vile mass warehousing of political refugees, I would have laughed in your face. The thought would have sent shivers up my spine. Today, I consider my years as an inmate as one of God's most precious gifts to me. A gift I value and cherish.

Recently, I've run across several verses in the Bible that speak of God's faithfulness. The more I thought about the word, the more I realized how jam-packed full of meaning it is. Yes, God never gives up on us. He is never any further than our outstretched arms can push Him away. Jesus never fails. But there is a whole other side to that coin. If you switch the syllables around, you might say that one who is faithful is full of faith. God has faith in us. Why else would He have gone to such drastic extremes to mend the tear in our relationship with Him through His Son? He thinks I'm worth the effort. God believes in me. Probably far more than I believe in myself. It makes me wonder, if my belief in Him has such dramatic eternal ramifications, how much more profound is His belief in me?

The day that I read the headline in the local paper, "Ex-pastor Sentenced to 3-10 Years," I thought that the world was coming to an end. Despair doesn't even begin to describe what was going through my head. Somehow, "at least I'm going to heaven" didn't cut it this time. In fact, I began to wonder if heaven was even my final destination at all. It has taken a lot of years to come to terms with what happened and I'm still dealing with the aftermath. More than once over the years I've shaken my fist at the sky crying the words, "Why God? Why?"

The Apostle Paul lists a litany of horrendous experiences he had, from shipwreck to stoning (2 Corinthians 11:25-30). I can't help but think that Paul too must have wondered at some point, "Why God? Why?" Some people just seem to have way too many bad things happen to them. Sometimes it's self-inflicted, but a lot of times tragedies come out of nowhere. Shouldn't we, the children of the King, have some kind of special cosmic brownie points? Maybe a get-out-of-jail-free card (or two)? I mean, even the cultists have tax-exempt status. There has to be more going on than meets the eye. Earlier, in the same writing, I think Paul hits the nail on the head when he writes, "But we have this treasure in jars of clay to show that this all-surpassing power is from God and not from us" (4:7). God's faith in us is so intimately intense that every difficulty, tragedy and trial is a gift with which we have been graciously entrusted. Maybe if He didn't care so much, we would be given free reign to jump to the head of the line. Maybe He believes in us so much, that He chooses to fill our baskets to overflowing, not just with rainbows and chocolate, but also with staggering pain and suffering because He knows exactly how far the rubber bands of our lives can stretch, and He wants us to experience the greatest heights, depth and breadth of His love.

I can honestly say that I like the man God has made me to be. I couldn't have said that twenty years ago. His grace is so much more precious to me. His forgiveness so much more profound. His polishing can be rigorous but the results are well worth it. My basket is overflowing with His mercy and purpose. Sometimes it's hard for me to understand why I have to be a Bipolar, Ex-con, Ex-Pastor recovering waiter. It's not a description that wins too much confidence on a resume. Nowadays, "Why God? Why?' has a whole different meaning to me.

It boggles my mind that out of all the gazillion people who have and will walk this earth, He wants to be my friend. This is the Guy who created **everything**, and He likes to hang out with ME. He enjoys my daily dramas and takes great pleasure in weaving all of the different colored threads of my day in to a tapestry, called my life. He rejoices when I rejoice. He weeps, when I weep. ME, the guy who took a perfectly well-potential life and turned it into a circus; ME, whose synapses misfire constantly causing all kinds of malfunctions, then He runs around and makes them good; ME, who has hurt too many unsuspecting bystanders by my selfishness. ME, who argues, connives and even resorts to threats sometimes during the holiness of prayer. Me. There is only one reason that I can come up with. There is only one reason that someone so Grand and Great would even bother with the likes of me, and my sorry attempts at holiness and devotion. Like a toddler's battered and beaten-up teddy bear, I am precious to Him, just because I am His.[5]

One Day

    I think, a long time ago, the world was a mess. A lot like the way it is now but without an escape clause. Before Jesus came, something really terrible happened. I don't completely understand what it was or why it was such a big deal, but apparently whatever exactly it was it was a big deal to God. When Adam and Eve committed the first sin by eating that fruit (and I really do hope it was tasty enough to be worth it), they became like turpentine on a beautifully painted mural. Things began to smear, and the end result was that the canvas looked nothing like what the Original Artist intended. I also think that as centuries passed, folks added their own personal graffiti to the Artist's work until the previous palette of colors got so covered that it no longer held any resemblance to its original form. In other words, I've come to believe that the Bible, which I consider to be 100% God's, is nothing close to the rulebook man makes it out to be. I think that's also true of religion. The Bible as a whole is a story, a story of God's love for man, a story of man's rejection of his Creator, and the consequences of choosing self over the true author of life. Enter: Jesus.
    The obvious solution would be to wipe the slate clean and start again. God did that once, and swore He would never do it again (Genesis 8:21). So along with the havoc man's sinfulness created, God had to contend with that darned gift of free will. A gift, which at times I'd rather do without but God clearly guards jealously. Please allow me to digress for just a moment to clarify something. I have absolutely no problem with the concept of The Trinity. If I've learned one thing on this ridiculously hard, though fascinating journey called life, God is just way too big to be limited to man's finite thinking. Really, with that kind

of enormity, even triune seems a little weak compared to all that He must be. Us trying to understand and define Him is really a hoot. It is also the root of so many problems that we face today. Free will on the other hand seems like handing an AK47 to a first-grader.

Back to the original point, the best resolution was one final sacrifice for the sin of mankind, but in order to maintain the integrity of the free will deal, the forgiveness had to be requested and received. What greater gift of love than for God to somehow become the sacrifice for us, to erase all of our disobedience as an incarnation of Himself. Considering the man made storylines on some soap operas, it's not such a far stretch. Oh, I should add too, I don't honestly believe that I've got this all right, but it all somehow fits in to God's enormous plan.

I find myself very grateful. All the time. I will, at times, almost unknowingly look up and say *thank you!* when even the simplest thing happens. It's kind of weird. It is totally genuine and it isn't forced, it just is. Have you ever really thought about grace, God's undeserved favor? I have been in several situations in my life where I found myself deeply destitute. Even something as simple as a toothbrush was like a miraculous gift from God Himself. There's something else you should probably know about me before you read any further. I can be a big jerk. And God's response to that incurable affliction is pretty much, "yeah, yeah, I know, now lets get to work." You're kidding me, right? Everyone else in my life eventually seems to come to the point of being sick of my ups and downs and ins and outs and gives up on me. God has to eventually throw up His hands, doesn't He? "No. Adam, I know everything there is to know about you. There is not a minute of the day that I am not standing at your side, cheering you on and lending a hand when its right. I love you, (even though, yes, by strict definition, you can be a big jerk)." Whether you are the loudest Bible thumper or the most devout atheist, if you can even slightly grasp this fact, this non-negotiable, mind-boggling, devastatingly frustrating fact, it changes everything. The fact that you are so completely, unabashedly, irrevocably loved, that there is nothing you can do to make God love you more or love you less cannot do anything but cause you to breathe a heartfelt thank you.

What I find most frustrating about all of it, is that I have to fight to stay connected to my reality, because like some dumb schmo, I keep trying to take back control. I've decided lately that I will not succumb to my own guilt either, because that's another trick I like to use to get the attention off of Him and on to Me. Then, the most incredible part of the whole thing is that this schlepping around the earth stuff and suffering the consequences of man's sin is only temporary. Right now He lives with us. One day, we will live with Him!

I have to say, I can't quite figure out what it is about self-rule that is so deeply preferential. It doesn't make sense. It's almost like I am infected by some mutating virus. Living under His Lordship is great. It should be a no-brainer. It is challenging and exhilarating. It makes you tired for bed at night, and awakens you with a stupid happy-grin on your face when you wake up. Demonstrating random acts of love is way better than a Percocet® high. But me, no thank you, I'd rather just swim in my own filth and struggle and complain. You see what I'm saying? It doesn't make sense. Its just too big of a gift. I printed a line from somewhere that I recently read and posted it on my bulletin board to help me deal with the guilt filled pity parties that I seem to like to throw. "We are not punished for the sin, but by the sin."

I understand theologically that Jesus fits the bill perfectly in God's grand world of grace, but how He fits in to my life is still somewhat confusing to me. Right now, He is at the invisible friend level, but much closer than friends. I like to imagine that He looks like Lucky Vanous from the old Diet Coke® commercials, but fully dressed and with longer hair, (having a good looking friend always makes you look better). As my roommate, I think that He and the cats should get together and help around the house a little bit when I'm at work. He thinks I'm funny. I appreciate His sense of humor too, and His persistent patience. I can't wait to meet Him face to face. First I'll probably get a big old hug, then a whack on the back of my head.

I am so very grateful that I am living in a time that the Church is moving away from traditionalism. What concerns me is that without traditions and rules, it is way too easy for God's grace and generosity to be abused, even trampled if you will. By expressing our freedom in Christ, as still-infected humans will inevitably, as history proves, morph our free-dom into a free-for-all. Grace is the most profound gift that can be given, and those three words that we all utter so quickly, "you are forgiven," cost our Heavenly Father a huge price. And it comes with responsibility. This perfect imaginary friend I cherish suffered a tremendous amount of pain, just so that when I mess up, God can say, "you are forgiven." My buddy, The Spirit whispers in my ear, "it's cool – forgiven and forgotten." I can't get the image out of my head what it would be like to hang, by my own weight (which is considerably more than Jesus'), in the hot Jerusalem sun, have my side ripped open and my innards flowing out, while the crying of my Mother and our friends can barely be heard over the laughter and taunting of the crowd. I feel like I hurt him when I revert to my jerky ways. He says, "you are forgiven."

One day this will all make sense. One day I will walk out of a mist and standing in front of me will be Jesus. I bet I even see a bit of myself in Him. One day I will look in to His eyes and it is just all gonna okay; every weakness transformed, every void filled. One day… I can only imagine…[6]

Draw Near

I'm thinking about Peter Brady, the middle son on "The Brady Bunch". He sang, "When it's time to change," and then his voice cracked during the chorus. It was pretty corny, even by early '70's standards. I have three specific thoughts about change. There is one kind that you sense deep within you, coming at you, about to re-arrange your life. Scary but hopeful. Then there is change that you know you need to initiate. After running around it and trying any other angle than the obvious, it is a matter of the will, of obedience, of surrender, of love. A little deeper than I like to go. And finally, change, although it can be an invigorating challenge, no matter what form it takes, it isn't potentially a whole lot of fun. It's a similar feeling to being cramped back in the seat of a sports car. You get out and unfold, eventually the muscle cramping gives way to a feeling of new found freedom where every stretch makes you feel at least three inches taller. Change.

It is my understanding that the offer of free salvation through Jesus' death and resurrection fulfilled a very specific prophecy written by the Prophet Jeremiah:
"The time is coming," declares the LORD,
"when I will make a new covenant
with the house of Israel
and with the house of Judah.
It will not be like the covenant
I made with their forefathers
when I took them by the hand
to lead them out of Egypt,

because they broke my covenant,
though I was a husband to them,"
declares the LORD.
This is the covenant I will make with the house of Israel
after that time," declares the LORD.
"I will put my law in their minds
and write it on their hearts.
I will be their God,
and they will be my people.
No longer will a man teach his neighbor,
or a man his brother, saying, 'Know the LORD,'
because they will all know me,
from the least of them to the greatest,"
declares the LORD.
"For I will forgive their wickedness
and will remember their sins no more.
Jeremiah 31:31-34

    My whole belief system is rooted in the fact that now God lives in my heart and doesn't have to give me a list of do's and don'ts; He writes His will on my heart and mind. Doing it by ritual and tradition just doesn't feel right to me. Freedom in Christ. Only problem is, I can't be trusted. I noticed something the other day that somehow escaped my eager eyes all of these years. While I am no longer under the law there is a matter of a personal law and that is what God promises to scribble into our lives. Grace, repentance, forgiveness, and all that great stuff doesn't mean that I am free to do as I wish. God finds His ways of getting His points across and there is, in fact, a law to which I am accountable. The one that is written on my heart and mind by the hand of my Creator and Best Friend.

    I am at a crossroad of change. Not the romantic coming in the wind kind. The change that I am staring in the eye is going to take every bit of concentration to make happen. More than that, since I've let the list get a little more than a little out of hand, I'm going to need to rest in God's grace and strength with a vengeance. My friend keeps telling me to "draw near." I'm sure it's very good advice. I'm just not sure how to do it. Wish I did because it sounds swell. I'm more of a talker, "okay, here we go, I'm walking out the front door, not sure which way to go to work today, trusting you to show me God…" I'm a baby - stepper-assure-me-each-step-of the-way kinda guy. I know I need to chill out, or, be still as it were. I guess I want to keep making sure He's there, watching, and filtering everything that happens through His satan-sifter. Really, you would think that He wouldn't keep making me feel like I'm clutching on to Him for dear life. For the sake of all of heaven's sanity, you wouldn't think He'd encourage this kind of behavior. But He does.

Worshipping the Lord is great. Sometimes the only thought that gets me through a frustrating shift at work is thinking about coming home and curling up in bed with The Word. Unfortunately, there is not always time and I'm not always thinking Jesus. I don't think that the 'be still and know that I am God' verse is necessarily just about getting quiet. There is an intended purpose for being still, knowing that God is God. Being still is a call to relationship. A ringing of the steeple bell. It's not an admonishment but an invitation. It's the same thing God asked Job after all of his whining and complaining, "Did you make all of this…?" God is in control, and I already have every spiritual blessing I could possibly need in Him. (Ephesians 1:3). Shut-up indeed.

My son has always been an old soul. When he was about three years old, we built an above ground pool in the backyard. Once the water was warm enough to tolerate, my daughter, a year older, and I, were in there swimming around like dolphins in the Florida sun. Chris, on the other hand, was a little more hesitant. He very calmly explained to us that he would rather wait until he had some safety-swimmies, maybe a mask and some fins. Always the saver, whereas my daughter and I will forever be a day late and a dollar short, he purchased a beginners swimming package at Toys R Us® the next day. That afternoon, as Ashley and I were splashing around, he climbed the pool's ladder fully prepared: swimmies, mask, flippers and even snorkel in full place. When he reached the top, he sat on the platform, feet dangling in the water, and there he stayed. In fact, there he stayed, in that exact spot, wearing all of his gear, every time we went swimming for the next three weeks. He wasn't upset. Didn't seem overly concerned, he simply explained that he wasn't ready yet. One afternoon, after another session of penny diving and raft races, he called me over and said, "Dad, I think I'm ready now…would give me a push?" I climbed out and said, "Okay Buddy, lets count to three. One…two…" "No Dad don't count, just do it!" So I did. I think sometimes, no matter how ready we think we are, a small push from our Father is exactly we need.

In prison, when you have to do something you don't want to do, one of the more popular encouragements is, "Man up!" The kind of intimacy that I have with Jesus can't help but to bring light things in my life that need changing, sometimes even by implosion. I'm grateful for that. I wouldn't want it any other way. I know too that lots of time, I just need to take a step in faith and God sends His legions of angels to make things a lot easier than I could have ever thought or imagined. I can't count on that though. Do I love God enough to let Him be God? Yes, I do. It's time to change.

Old Friends

I have always had a strangely intense fascination with the Titanic. I'm not really sure why. Years before the Leonardo DiCaprio movie made a splash at the box office, I was a member of The Titanic Historical Society©. I remember how excited I was when the ship's wreckage was finally discovered. Then my sense of astonishment as eerie pictures of its remains surfaced from the ocean floor. If I believed in reincarnation it would be a fair assumption that my previous life had something to do with the behemoth's demise. Wherever the impression was made, somewhere along the way, Titanic's tale made its impression. The irony was not lost to me either when my teenaged daughter was similarly captivated by Hollywood's version, opening her eyes for the first time to the reality of eternity. I knew, of course, that there was no Jack or Rose in the real-life epic. They were characters invented to romanticize the true horror of that night almost a hundred years ago, yet the message of the modern day film was profound nonetheless. For months, you couldn't listen to the radio without hearing Celine Dion singing the theme song "My Heart Will Go On."[7]

Over the last few weeks, I have been trying to wrap my brain around a question that I can barely put into words. I've found myself initiating conversations on the subject and trying over and over to verbalize what seems to be an elemental concept which inevitably short circuits my synapses, leaving me feeling foolishly impotent. Basically, I'm trying to figure out, if love has a beginning, does it have an end? It doesn't take much to fairly well pinpoint a place of origin. whether that be a first meeting or introduction, a revelation or even a discovery. That makes sense. The part that makes my cerebellum throb is trying to conceptualize an end. The very definition of love seems to demand that it cannot stop. I understand that love can be damaged or challenged or even regretted, but once birthed, can genuine love really die? Is it that the most important concept in the universe is being mis-identified, or is the very essence of our Creator, in which we are privileged to share, being thwarted by self-indulgent human parameters? Have we become a society so corrupted by the ravages of sin that emotional homicide is not only acceptable but preferable, as long as it protects our heart?

I am sitting here at my desk, looking at several translations of 1 Corinthians 13:4-7. Paul's definition of love, and I am seeing a very clear and obvious common principal found in each. From The King James version to The Living Bible, one word is screaming it's presence. A common thread that links and unites all of the phrases and adjectives. Acceptance. Love is the unconditional, unrelenting, unflappable acceptance of the person to whom it is directed. No matter what, why, where, when or how, the object of love is never diminished or considered any less regardless of the circumstance. It puts the others' needs and desires above its own. It is an immutable fact, a force in and of itself that allows for weakness and fault. It grows stronger through difficulty, as it is stretched beyond the limits of human feeling and emotion. It stands as a definition not a motive. It is kind and patient, never jealous, boastful, proud or rude. It isn't selfish or quick-tempered. It keeps no record of wrongs, rejoices in truth, not in evil. It is always supportive, loyal and hopeful (CEV). It is acceptance of the whole, beyond reason and feeling. And, it never fails.

God is love. It helps me a lot to know that He loves me, no matter what. It can't be an easy task all the time. The other thing about love is that it always forgives. I don't have to earn it. I don't have to beg or plead or jump through hoops. I am forgiven for one reason, because He loves me. Sometimes I get caught up in the weakness of my humanity and I start to think that if I don't go to church, or I don't read my Bible enough or if I neglect to give Him the attention that He deserves, that He thinks less of me, or that He's mad at me. I forget that love is who He is. He cannot be anything else. I'm sure that when I get caught up in my own self-involved logic it causes Him hurt. I hope that when I give Him His due it makes Him smile. Really, where can I flee from His presence? If I go up to the heavens He's there, if I make my bed in the depths He's there. If I rise on the wings of the dawn or settle on the far side of the sea, even there His hand guides me, His right hand holds me fast. (Psalm 139:7-10). God is love.

I have a son and a daughter. Never, in a million years, could I have imagined that I would have the capacity to feel for them even the slightest of what God feels for me, but I do. It's funny, sometimes they treat me like I treat my Heavenly Father: an afterthought, an intrusive burden or just an overwhelming sentiment. They call every now and then, but they are more interested with their own lives than in mine. The fact that I have become an extra instead of a featured player to them hurts me deeply, nonetheless if they were to call me at two o'clock in the morning and say they needed me, I'd be there in a heartbeat. I understand why The Prodigal Son's Dad gave up his fortune. I would do anything I could to make their lives better, including leave them alone. I could not fathom anything that they could ever do or say that would change my love for them. It's all very "Cat's In the Cradle.".[8]

What started me thinking about the lifespan of love was not God's love for me. That's a given. In fact the more I thought about it, the more I realized how much I take the magnitude of His unconditional love for me for granted. What got me going on the subject is that I am haunted by people in my past who once claimed to love me, but if questioned today would probably espouse an unequivocal, "oh, him?" The problem I have, is that I still have love for them, and I miss the impact that their unique characters had on my life. I began to wonder what happened that would put us at such very opposite ends of the spectrum. Why their decion to close the door outweighs my desire to keep it open. Why do I still accept them, but they do not accept me? I wondered if it's because I'm more needy of love than they are, but the facts don't bare that truth. It's definitely not a case of me being a better person, in fact I'd argue that it's just the opposite. Did the hurt or pain that I unintentionally inflicted somehow cut deeper than the scars they left on me. I don't think so. Thwarted love leaves pretty pronounced wounds.

I've done some horrendously awful things, and God has forgiven me for every single one. Even as I type the words I shake my head in wonder and awe. Forgiven. Completely. I am accepted without reservation, every scar, every wound, every hurt. The mind-boggling forgiveness and grace that God has so lavishly poured into my life really allows me no other option. If I were to choose not to forgive then how could I receive the tremendous love that God has for me? Forgiveness extended to others allows me to receive forgiveness for myself. I think that maybe the reason some people refuse to forgive, and therefore stifle love is not because they are bad or weak, but because opening that door would flood their hearts with a vulnerability that they are unwilling to embrace. No doubt, unconditional love is an emotional risk. Not one I would ever *choose* to take. Remember the woman that anointed Jesus' head and feet with costly perfume? She is still remembered as a societal outcast, a harlot. Even to this day her sinful life qualifies our memory of her. Yet Jesus commended her as one who loved greatly, because she was forgiven greatly (Luke 7:47).

I guess the conclusion I've come to is that love doesn't so much end as it can become obscured by unforgiveness. Psychologically, cancelling one's interpersonal debts is powerful and healing stuff.[9] It's a huge relief of unnecessary emotional baggage. On a spiritual level however, it is the difference between our eternal life and death. That's not to say that forgiving someone is always easy or that it doesn't take time to achieve. I believe that God's Word is a romance novel. From Genesis to Revelation, it is a central theme that can't be ignored. The Bible is a story of God's patience, acceptance, forgiveness, and love.

I can't tell you why God has been so generous to me, not only by extending such ferocious forgiveness, but also by allowing me to marinate in some of life's most fetid sewage. A lot of people don't have that privilege. The magnitude of His bounty couldn't be more obvious to me than if it were to explode in my face. I can't say that I would have ever in a million years chosen the path that my life has taken, or that I enjoyed even a minute of the years spent behind bars, or confined to institutions, or hiding under my bed sobbing and begging God to let me die, or the intense pain of knowing how badly I've hurt and disappointed those I love. But I am grateful. Grateful to be forgiven so absolutely, grateful to be at the tail end of it all, and grateful that today's trials are tomorrows victories.

If I speak with human eloquence and angelic ecstasy but don't love, I'm nothing but the creaking of a rusty gate. If I speak God's Word with power, revealing all his mysteries and making everything plain as day, and if I have faith that says to a mountain, "Jump," and it jumps, but I don't love, I'm nothing. If I give everything I own to the poor and even go to the stake to be burned as a martyr, but I don't love, I've gotten nowhere. So, no matter what I say, what I believe, and what I do, I'm bankrupt without love. Love never gives up. Love cares more for others than for self. Love doesn't want what it doesn't have. Love doesn't strut, doesn't have a swelled head, doesn't force itself on others, isn't always "me first," doesn't fly off the handle, doesn't keep score of the sins of others, doesn't revel when others grovel, takes pleasure in the flowering of truth, puts up with anything, trusts God always, always looks for the best, never looks back, but keeps going to the end. Love never dies.

1 Corinthians 12:1-8 THE MESSAGE

Weapons of Mass Destruction

God and I are fighting. Probably if I had any kind of intelligence I wouldn't even waste the time or energy. It doesn't take a brain surgeon to know who is going to win. I just find Him so frustrating sometimes. Usually when we go at it, it's about the same thing. He refuses to do what I want Him to do, or at least within the time frame that makes most sense to me. There was an off-Broadway show several years ago titled, "Your Arms Are Too Short to Box With God."[10] I'm still not convinced.

Like I said, we've had this battle many times before. Inevitably I cave, but not without a fight. A lot of times He will miraculously intervene one way or another, not necessarily the way that I expect, but then I feel like a fool for ever having started the feud. I've spent years at a time angry with God. He's never for a minute stopped loving me. I have noticed that our skirmishes have become less and less lately. I'm guessing that one of us is mellowing with age. This particular conflict is a humdinger. I am staging an all-out multi-cause protest. I've yelled, I've screamed, I've cried, I've negotiated and I've even threatened, but He is just not budging. He can be so stubborn sometimes. I'm never especially happy when we are embroiled in war. I miss my friend Jesus, but everyone knows that you can't consort with the enemy. The objective side of my brain understands that I need to get off of my high horse and just surrender to His loving care and impeccable timing. He's never failed me before. I need to say I'm sorry and allow His vitamin-rich purposes nourish my sole. I need to say, so-long self and appreciate that He cares enough to infuriate me. Right now I can't. The whole situation has me inconsolably depressed.

The other day I was looking at my daughter's myspace™ page. She has a scrolling collage of baby pictures that draw me in every time. I took most of them. In fact, the only one I didn't take was the last one. I was in jail. The trust of her childlike father-worship had been shattered by the time that picture was taken. Her innocence was gone. When the montage began to roll for a second time, I found myself apologizing to the little girl playing on the beach, opening birthday presents, dressed up for Christmas and cuddling her favorite blanket. The experience was incredibly heart wrenching, and wet. It was, however, the last image that was the one that was left burned in my brain. My precious daughter smiling on the outside, but crushed on the inside. Riding the carousel of my daughter's childhood made me wonder how God feels when He looks at my spiritual *myspace* page. What is the most memorable image He sees when He closes my page for the day?

I've been fighting with God all of my life. It hasn't always been quite as obvious as the screaming match of late, but I can look back and see that my life has been filled with all kinds of weapons of warfare. Every pill I've popped, every selfish direction I've chosen and every mile I've run screams a battle cry. I learned at a very early age the benefits of running, the emotional value of putting distance between myself and my problems. When I was growing up, every night my Mom would cook my Dad and me a delicious gourmet meal and then disappear into the bathroom before she served. When she returned she looked like she had walked through a windstorm. Apparently she was having a secret tryst with a certain Mr. Jack Daniels. Although we could never find the bottle, her slurred speech and annoyingly saccharine behavior spoke volumes. My dad spent all of his free time in the two greenhouses he'd built in the backyard. Here he would cultivate his prize winning collection of bromeliad plants (think pineapple tops) day after day and night after night. When he wasn't there, he would be at the office captaining a paint and hardware distribution business he'd founded. Mom's inebriating affair was undoubtedly the inspiration for much of his success.

A YEAR FOR DAD

I learned early at an early age that it's easier to run than fight. A big part of my childhood was spent hiding alone in my bedroom. When I was 16 my act hit the road. I was an apprentice at a nearby summer stock theatre and chosen to be William Shatner's personal assistant. One night, I got frustrated or angry or something and walked out. The show he was performing in was supposed to go to Broadway the following year. It was an opportunity I didn't want to miss. When I called the theatre the next day to apologize and try to get my job back, I was told that I had already been replaced. It was a hard lesson. When the show closed quicker than it opened, it provided little solace. My act of rebellion had its consequences.

Thinking about all the ways we battle with God, I realize that I am not alone in my heavenly hostilities. Adam and Eve played hide and seek, Jacob wrestled, David dallied, Jonah took up residence in the belly of a fish, Paul tortured the innocent, and on and on and on. In modern times we hide behind doctrines and causes and we unfairly condemn and judge. Sometimes we even try to be God's emissary with agendas of our own justifications and rationalizations. I guess it's really no wonder that from Genesis to Revelations the theme of war is so prominent. It must all hurt God's heart terribly.

If any message comes through crystal clear from the history of man's relationship with God, it's that we are all casualties of war. We never seem to learn. Yet God allows it to continue. Certainly He could have nuked our pathetic attempts millennia ago, but He hasn't. Perhaps there are benefits to fighting that we don't see until all the bloodshed is in the past. Perhaps there is good reason that He allows us to battle on ground that already belongs to Him. When we are asked to join the Lord's army, He's not looking for robots and automatons. He requires soldiers of conviction and steadfast heart. I've often suggested to parents who have raised their children in traditions of the faith that it's okay when their children "rebel" and choose their own way. We all need to be saved from **something**, or else salvation has little meaning. Maybe if God is not the winner, then everyone loses.

I have no doubt that whether He does what I want Him to do or not, I will eventually end up on my knees in gratitude and I will walk away from the whole sordid mess better, stronger and more convinced than ever that He needs to be in charge. For me not to wrestle with Him would be wrong because I need to lose as much as I need to fight. I need to be broken. I need His mercy and His grace to envelope my soul. I need to need Him. And He needs to be God, firmly enthroned, my King of Kings, Lord of Lords.

Mr. Nice Guy

I am someone people usually feel comfortable being around. I really don't come off as a threat or aggressively imposing. Folks seem at ease randomly saying hello and making eye contact with me. I'm easy to talk to and a good listener. I'm the person that the clerk at the gas station remembers and the lady at the deli counter has no problem throw me an extra slice or two of swiss cheese with a wink and a smile. I wouldn't say that I'm especially good-looking, probably comfortable would be a better description. Chances are, if you were to ask someone if they knew me, they would say, "Oh yeah. Adam. He's a nice guy." Old ladies think I'm a sweetheart. Customers find me charming and amusing. Teenagers think I'm cool. That's me, Mr. Nice Guy. A likeable, easy-going good old boy scamp that everyone considers their best friend.

I don't mean to say that it's a sham, or at all insincere. Really though, I don't think I'm such a nice guy. Sometimes I think I carry the burdens of others to avoid feeling the weight of my own. I throw the best pity-parties in town! I get so jealous of people who seem to instinctively know how to play the game of life. I feel so lost so much of the time. Hanging on for dear life. On my myspace™ page, under the heading, "People I'd like to meet" I entered something that people have told me they think is just adorable. I mean it with all of my heart: *Everyone seems to know stuff about life that I dont. I figure that there's some guy who was in charge of giving out manuals and forgot to issue one to me.* I feel so guilty so much of the time that people see me as just a good-old boy. Rarely is Child of God the definition by which I am qualified, though it is the one I'd prefer. When it comes right down to it, I think I spend more time allowing others' opinions and standards dictate who I am, than being true to the man I think I should be. I'm so good at being a nice guy that no one can even tell that sometimes it feels like I'm just spewing a lot of smoke and mirrors. Truthfully, putting others first is exhausting. If the Creator of everything that is, was, and is to be loves me, Adam, with such ferocity, shouldn't that be enough for me? My self-worth shouldn't come from anywhere but heaven; from being His child, His representative. Instead I'm out there shaking hands and kissing babies. No, I really don't think I should be thought of as such a nice guy at all.

God's Word has to contain a message that goes beyond the confines of societies and civilizations since He has assured that it be around for so long. Really, most of the stories themselves have little to do with my life in the 21st Century. I can't tell you the last time I muzzled an ox or caught fish and cooked it over an open fire. As I daily strive to work out my salvation with fear and trembling, I am more and more convinced that to approach the Bible as a book of rules and lists is a complete misunderstanding of what God intended. I think it misconstrues the whole point, and just doesn't make sense. When I look beyond the details and see the bigger picture, the theme is clear: God's relationship with man. Every story, every narrative, every Psalm and every parable points to our relationship with Him. The very fact that He comes to live in our hearts and orchestrates our lives clearly indicates that His interest in us is relational. What happened in the Garden of Eden was not as much a behavioral deal breaker as it was a relational desecration. My relationship with Him is the filler of the gap that I try so hard to stuff with others' approval. When I think about the times that I am struggling the most, it is when I want something else to fulfill a need that only He can. I never feel good enough, or faithful enough, or diligent enough. I feel like I fall so short of what I think He expects of me. When I'm not liking Him so much, on the deepest level, it's because I think He's not so thrilled with me. The Apostle Paul expressed it perfectly when he said, "the good I want to do, I cannot do…oh wretched man that I am." It's the same trap I'm in today, but as long as I'm a nice guy, everything is a-okay.

To have a relationship with Christ is to be identified with Him in every part of my being. When I was married, and I must confess that to some extent it still pops up today, wherever I would go, or whatever I would do or talk about I carried a part of my wife with me. The stories I would tell, the decisions I would make, just about everything included her, because she was so very much a part of who I was. Should my relationship with Christ be anything less? I am aftererall the bride to His groom.

I've been feeling so very ineffective and purposeless in my walk with Jesus lately. Just a failure. I've been wondering why I'm not moving mountains or preaching messages of salvation to the masses. Why all I seem to be is some nice guy, and not even very good at that. Sitting on my couch the other night, watching some re-run I've seen a hundred times, I remembered the 86 cents I gave to someone at the convenience store because they were short at the register. I thought about the hysterical call I got from the co-worker who needed to blow off steam and thanked me for being there to listen and help put things in perspective. I remembered the look of the little old lady I passed on the street when I smiled and nodded my head at her. Other little snippits popped in and out of my head of the past week and I thought how natural each action was for me. I didn't plan or think them through. I didn't struggle to obey some oppositional command. It was just me, being a nice guy. It felt right.

I may never get to accomplish the lofty goals that I daydream about. Perhaps its really not the grand overtures of love and faith that God has designed for me. I think maybe what I'm called to is a personal, intimate, minute-by-minute relationship with Jesus, a man, just like myself who touched lives and healed hearts one by one, encounter by encounter. It all makes me wonder if this likeable persona by which I'm perceived is more than just a cry for acceptance. Perhaps God, knowing my innate needs has chosen to use a weakness as an opportunity for His strength. Maybe my efforts to be that likable fella, easy to talk to and always ready to go the extra mile is really an expression of His life in me.

    I was reading the other day about the crowds that followed Jesus around and sat in the blazing sun to listen to Him talk. I thought about how a lot of them were there just for a free meal, hunger being far more important to them than spiritual nourishment. Jesus had to know that all of their motives were not completely noble and pure, but it didn't stop Him. The scraps of bread and chunks of fish they each received were a personal gift to each and every recipient. I would dare say that their lives were never the same again. I think if I ever met Jesus on the street, I'd like Him. I don't think He would be all flashy and smooth-talking. I bet we'd sit on a park bench together eating chocolate Carvel ice cream in sugar cones. He would give me an extra napkin as I attempted to keep the chocolate from dripping down my chin. It would be fun and I would probably like Him, just because He was a nice guy.

Hard Candy Is Still Candy

    I am broke. I am always broke. I don't just mean sometimes, I mean just about every day. And I'm not talking about the kind of broke where all you have left in your wallet is a ten dollar bill, or the kind when you're short on cash but have plenty of plastic to get you through. I'm talking about the kind of broke where my net worth is all of about seventeen cents, if you count the pennies under the sofa cushions and the hope of passing off some of the petrified skittles under there as precious gems at a pawnshop. I hate it. I used to get really jealous of people who go shopping for sport. Shopping to me is a painful experience that provides the single pleasure of maybe, just maybe, being able to afford a pack of Rolaids. When I ask people how they can afford such extravagances as having more in their house to drink than tap water, one word always resounds back. Credit. Now, since I am chronically credit-impaired, which sounds so much better than irresponsible with money, I have to operate on cold hard cash. When I was just serving at the restaurant, I had cash coming in every day. If I couldn't afford something today, chances are I would be able to in a day or two. Now that I'm in salary mode, I need to plan and budget. A sure recipe for disaster. I'm not sweatin' it though. I've noticed that there is a fine line between denial and surrender.

    What's the worst that could happen? They throw me in debtor's prison? Frankly, the simplicity of prison life is something I sometimes kind of miss. All of it is just a reminder to me that everyone of my days is written in His book before one of them came to be (Ps. 139: 16). I already know how the book of my life starts, and how it ends, my job now is to just sit back and enjoy the process as the Big Guy writes the chapters in between. Maybe offer Him a plot twist every now and then. Really, in God's heart, it's all a done deal anyway. I'm cool with that. Even when I am at my most ridiculous, He is always there, standing on His tiptoes at the back of the crowd waving me down, like a proud parent after a school play, making His presence known. Over and over He reveals His faithfulness and grace and love. Oftentimes in a language that is unique to only He and I. I have had to start over from scratch so many times that the trappings of wealth no longer have much hold on me. I couldn't tell you the last time I bought a piece of clothing anywhere but Goodwill. I grew up privileged and took for granted all the luxuries. Nowadays if I have shampoo, enough toilet paper to get by and maybe some Chinese food every now and then, I pretty much consider myself to be living large. I'm tired of unnecessary complications, because, somehow, as great as it is to be living with all the conveniences of the 21st Century, it's way too easy to get distracted. I used to think that nuns and monasteries were ridiculous inventions of a misguided religious system, but I have to wonder, what kind of freedom does freedom really inspire?

I've been thinking a lot about the concept of time lately. Although my brain does sort of start to short circuit when I try to grasp the idea that not such thing as time exists for God. I expect that the haze will clear on that subject when we are gathered in His presence. If the existence of mankind were a line, why did God choose to step in to history at the specific point that He did I wonder. You would think that what with the internet and cable and cell phones, now would have been a better time than 2000 years ago. One appearance on *The Tonight Show* would have certainly been more productive and cost-effective than the door to door approach. Much less wear and tear on the sandals too. The only answer that I can come up with is that the simplicity of the times was exactly the reason that Jesus appeared on the scene when He did, and it confirms to me all the more what my heart has been saying all along. Individual, personal, initimate, relationship is the key. He wasn't in the least bit interested in numbers.

When Jesus spoke, He touched hearts, hearts that were not distracted by a million different philosophies, or intellectualized theories or endless possessions. In fact, it seems that every Gospel points to the fact that the more distracted a person was, the harder it was to accept The Message (Luke 18:25). The scholarly Pharisees are a good case in point. Jesus words, "Let the little children come to me, and do not hinder them, for the kingdom of God belongs to such as these" is like a message in a bottle for His believers of this millennium.

Imagine the typical Sunday morning church service. A man steps up to the pulpit and reads from The Word. His authority and heartfelt words hang over the crowd like the overpowering fragrance of a grove of lilacs on a summer day. A hush settles over the congregation. You can hear a pin drop. All of a sudden, a man who you have sat next every week for over a year stands up and begins aggressively threatening the man on stage. With a calm reserve, and a loving voice, the speaker simply says, "Be quiet. Come out of him." The heckler shrieks. A blood curdling, stomach wrenching, guttural sound you have never heard before. In most churches, it would be at this point that the ushers would step forward and escort the now deflated figure from the room. While everyone watches them drag his limp body from the pew, you turn around and see the man on stage standing there with a tear rolling down his cheek, looking almost as if he'd lost his best friend. I don't think that the story Mark tells in His Gospel (1:21-28) paints the picture of a self-righteous Savior who is angry at the man for interrupting Him, or feels glad that He handled the scene with such dramatic aplomb. I believe that we are meeting a Man who is hurt by the condition of His creation and longs for the day that He can gather each and every one of His children under His wings, wipe their tears and give them a big old bear hug.

Isaiah says that, "He had no beauty or majesty to attract us to him, nothing in his appearance that we should desire him" (Isaiah 53:2). Jesus was no rock star. This was a man who literally carried His heart on His sleeve and the weight of the world on His shoulders. His punishment, crushing and piercing, was not just physical. This was a man of compassion, and sorrows, our sorrows, someone who really cared about each individual heart that he encountered. Mark's first chapter overflows with this reality, from Simon's mother-in-law, to the guy with leprosy. I'd even bet that when the man He healed did just the opposite of what he was instructed by telling his story all over town, Jesus wasn't in the least bit annoyed. I can see Him smiling and shaking His head as He planned His next move. Leprosy was not the only ailment healed that day. Jesus filled a need in the man's soul that ran so deep that he had no choice but to hoop and holler and give his Healer the glory. A much needed and longed for relationship had been restored. There was no need for the now healthy man to Google™ an explanation or scientifically define what had happened. He had been healed, body, soul and spirit, and everyone had to know.

I have this hunch that the first time I stand before my Lord, and look in to His eyes, I am not only going to experience all the love that I have spent my earthly life longing for, but I think that I will recognize the gaze looking back at me and realize how truly familiar it is. I will recognize His surprisingly familiar voice, and warm memories will rush into my thoughts of remembrance. I will take in to my heart a feeling of peace and comfort that I have only experienced in bits and pieces throughout my lifetime. There will be no distractions. Honestly, I can't wait.

So the holiday season approaches and I have no idea how I will afford any of it, even the smallest token to my kids. I have a bunch of people I'd like to bless, just for being a part of my life. The same people who inevitably, usually unknowingly, have been used by God to reveal His purposes for me. I wish I could give everyone I love one of those snippets I mentioned earlier. Perhaps just 10 minutes of distraction free time, enough to experience God's faithfulness, His mercy, and His love; a memory of familiarity to draw upon when they too bask in the tenderness of His gaze and the intimacy of His smile. I love to give books that mean something to me as gifts. I usually do a lot of shopping on Amazon™ at Christmas, but I can't afford that this year. Maybe one of the reasons that Jesus told the leprosy-guy to keep it all to himself was because He knew that a transformed life speaks far more volumes than excited words. Paul even refers to our lives as living epistles. Yes, it may be sparse pickings under the tree this year, if there even is a tree, but I think I know what I can give. I've been inspired by one of my favorite characters in The Bible. An unsung hero. There isn't much written about the boy who gave His lunch from which Jesus fed over 5,000. All that we do know is that he gave all that he had to give. I have always been impressed by that kid. He gave crumbs and nourished thousands. "…whoever welcomes a little child like this in my name welcomes me."

Bread and fish for everyone!

Home Is Where The Heart Is

I am a dreamer. I always have been. During my childhood and teen years I spent a lot of time visiting a whole other world of my own creation in my head. I hesitate to admit, that it's only been in the last few years that I've stopped going there on an almost daily basis. Checking in to my alternate reality in my adult years had been my method for falling asleep. My other life is everything my real life isn't. It's a great place. It's a safe-haven where I am loved and secure and completely accepted. Where my talents are appreciated and I have lots of friends. It's a place where I make a difference and all of my bills are paid. I'm really good-looking there too. I miss going there sometimes. I think God knows how much I like visiting because He has let me holiday there on a few occasions, in dreams, even though we both know it's not the most healthy place for me to linger.

Not only am I a physical dreamer, but I am also a lucid dreamer. Wikipedia[11], the online encyclopedia defines lucid dreams like this: *A lucid dream is a dream in which the person is aware that he or she is dreaming while the dream is in progress, also known as a conscious dream. When the dreamer is lucid, he or she can actively participate in the dream environment without any of the inhibitions or limitations that otherwise would feel natural to persons who incorrectly believe they are in the "real" waking world. Lucid dreams can be extremely real and vivid depending on a person's level of self-awareness during the lucid dream.* Lucid dreams are awesome. I used to have them a lot more regularly than I do now, mostly during a period of my life that I needed to escape reality. That's why I think that God blesses me with the ability to go there every now and then too. It's His very intimate and personal way of hugging me. I've done some reading on the subject of lucid dreams and even learned some tricks that I can use when I'm there. If I'm not sure if I'm dreaming or not, because it feels so real, I throw my legs out behind me. If I float I know it's a dream. Of course if I ever felt the need to use this test in real life, I'd fall flat on my tail and probably end up in a hospital, possibly a psychiatric one. I've also learned that if I want a dream to continue I can spin myself in circles. If I don't like the situation I'm in, I just have to shake my head to wake up. That definitely doesn't work in real life. I've tried.

I recently re-read one of my favorite entries in one of my favorite devotionals The day's message was a challenge to the reader to determine whether or not his last request in prayer represented a personal cause or a personal devotion to his Creator. It got me thinking. I believe that the Bible is all about God's relationship with man and I believe that Jesus lived, died and rose from the dead to heal that relationship that had been broken. If life is all about my relationship with God, am I motivated by dwelling in His presence or by living an alternate reality that is really no reality at all?[12]

After a very specific and detailed discourse on practical living, one of the few recorded in fact, Jesus sums up His teaching with the statement. "Where your treasure is, there your heart will be also" (Matthew 6:21). I know people who are incredible storytellers. They can weave a tale with such colorful detail that by the time they get to the end, you feel as if you've just gotten off of a roller coaster. I, however, am a firm believer in short-handing unnecessarily drawn-out experiences. When I get in to a disagreement with someone, I'd rather avoid all of the emotional hoo-ha and just settle the matter and move on. 'I was wrong', 'you were wrong,' 'this is how we can fix it' kind of thing. The crowds listening to Jesus that day in the blazing Middle-Eastern sun were probably getting restless by the time He made this statement. They had heard about salt, light, murde, adultery, divorce, generosity, fasting, prayer, etc. If I had been there that day, I probably would have been the guy in the crowd who was shaking his head in his hands and finally blurting out, "Lord, can we just cut to the chase!" Jesus did, with a statement so intensely heart rending that I imagine for a few minutes afterwards, all you could hear was the wind whipping through the trees. Eugene Peterson in The Message version translates the verse, "The place where your treasure is, is the place you will most want to be, and end up being."

There is an interesting dichotomy taught in the New Testament. On one hand, Jesus spent His life hanging out with the common folk and society's most wretched. On the other hand, Paul says that bad company corrupts good morals. The Apostle John also has a lot to say about how bad it is to love the world. Are we, as God's children supposed to hang out on the street corners wearing a Hazmat suit? I don't think our message would be especially appealing if we did. It is the citizenship of our heart that gives us all of the necessary protective armor that we could possibly need to be participants in a world so stained by sin. We are to have a relationship with the world in which our lives are the influence, not vice versa. I love the Psalmists description. He describes God as a dwelling place, a rich and fertile land where we are nourished, strengthened and protected. A place where our cup overflows and goodness and loving kindness follow us around everywhere we go. Its kind of dream-like.

When I have no idea how I'm going to make my next car payment, and my daughter won't answer my calls, and I can't imagine a time when I will ever be happy again, it's the dwelling place of my heart that keeps it all in perspective. I wonder sometimes if God gets tired of hearing me whine and complain. I've tried approaching Him with the suggestion that if He would just take care of thus-and-such His life would be so much easier. I would quiet down and maybe He could even get a day off every now and then. Play golf, create a galaxy or two, whatever. Truth is though, according to the Scriptures, it's not my complaining that concerns Him. It's when I stop complaining and decide to take matters in to my own hands that bothers Him the most.

Sometimes it feels like dwelling in God is like trying to hold on to a merry-go-round that is spinning out of control; holding on for dear life while all of the riders are flung off one by one. Belief is so much easier than faith. Belief is cuddly and safe. Faith requires a trust, and an anchoring in waters that are sometimes fickle and dangerous. It can be a harrowing ride.

One of the first steps a potter must take to begin the process of molding his clay on the wheel, is to assure that it is adhered and centered. For the clay, it's a grueling experience of being pulled and crushed, squeezed and flattened. The artist can do nothing unless this process is fully explored. Dwelling in the presence of God can be mind-numbingly distressing when every ounce of our being is shouting, "foul ball!" Some of the greatest men of God experienced the worst that life could possibly offer and rose victorious. It's no wonder that in one of Paul's most powerful writings he exhorts his readers to "Rejoice in the Lord always. Again I say: Rejoice!" and then goes on to tell them, in very practical terms, how to deal with life's inevitable anxieties. (Phillipians 4:4-9)

No matter what is happening around me, as long as my heart is dedicated to the true reality, I cannot fall. If God is for me, who can be against me? When all is said and done, I have to ask myself, what is the primary priority of my life? What kind of treasures matter to me the most? Dwelling in my Creator isn't always a panorama of beautiful flowing streams and fields of wildflowers. It isn't always sunny and it doesn't always feel so great. That's okay. It's home, and Home is where my heart is.

Heaven I Think.

I've been sort of obsessed with eternity lately. And mortality. There is just way too much craziness in my life right now. I think I'm starting to look forward to escaping this particular reality. I wish I understood more what to expect. That being said, I've been re-reading Rob Bell's Velvet Elvis[13]. I tend to do that, read stuff over and over. I think it comes from limited library access and cherishing week old newspapers in jail. Basically, the title, (the meaning of which I couldn't figure out until I read the first chapter), has a powerful message in and of itself. Before I explain, may I suggest that you add this book to your Someday-List. The story goes, something like, he finds a painting of Elvis on black velvet in his basement, or attic. As he looks at the flourished signature of the painter at the bottom, he proposes in his mind that it is the last painting ever to be painted in the world. That the artist established that his South Jersey rendition of The King of Rock 'N Roll is the ultimate painting that none other could exceed. Painters put down your brushes. Then he takes that whole train of thought and throws it at why it is not good that the Body of Christ remain stagnant in their seeking of God's truth. Just as the craft of painting evolves, so does our need to fervently seek what God is saying today as opposed to living for Christ with a 21st Century world mentality and an 1890 belief system. Our ability to perceive God's enormity and how He both relates and wishes to relate with us within the realities of our today is the key. The idea of sociology and how our race has mentally evolved since the beginning of time fascinates me. I think about it a lot.

So I decided just before Christmas, since I had to skip the holiday, I would read the whole New Testament in The Message version before New Years. Saturday is Valentine's Day. I should be done with Hebrews by the weekend. Actually I did a little skipping around and I decided to end the commitment and return to my trusty NIV after reading just one more Gospel. I picked Luke. Peterson's chapter introduction is amazing. It inspires you to look at it from a completely fresh angle. This whole thing is starting to get real to me. Now, I love my Bible, but in all honesty, it is sometimes like re-reading a People magazine from 1983. Something I actually do sometimes enjoy doing, but much prefer more current editions. So, I'm wondering, with all the *funny-fundies* still rampant in the streets, the folks screaming "King James or die," how far am I willing to break down the barriers of traditionalism and forge a path in my faith that is uniquely mine and God's? To live a life that other Christians might poo-poo, but those outside of the faith respect and admire. The reality is that I break down the barriers "unofficially" all the time. But in theory, I think it's important that I take into account the experiences of other smarter, wiser, more experienced folks too. It all comes down to which song does God prefer that I sing, *How Great Thou Art* or *You 'da Man, God*?

My thoughts about the apostle Paul have changed a lot since my maze through The Message too. I like him a lot better now. I understand him better. I wonder when he became so knowledgeable about God's desires. Did it all happen on Damascus road? The description gets bigger every time you read about it in Acts, but by 2 Corinthians, you start to thinking it was all a little more complex than just a flash of light. "I know a man, in Christ who fourteen years ago – whether in the body I do not know, or whether out of the body I do not know, God knows – such a one was caught up to the third heaven. And I know such a man - whether in the body I do not know, or whether out of the body I do not know, - how he was caught up in to Paradise and heard inexpressible words, which is not lawful for a man to utter." (2 Corinthians 12:3,4). Then by Thessalonians he pretty well shows his hand by giving away all kinds of detail about coming events. (2 Thessalonians 2). He was one plugged in fella. Paul has a great resume, I should probably heed his words right? 86 the forging ahead stuff? I think the idea I like best about eternity with God is that I am counting on the fact that it's all going to be so much easier there than it is here. Or maybe we'll all have personal assistants.

I fulfilled a fantasy this week. It was a way bigger deal to me than I thought it would be. The rightness or wrongness of my decision not withstanding, God spoke to me very clearly about His opinion on the matter. There was even a dream about it a week before. I don't do the prophetic dream thing. I really want to, but so far, as much fun as dreams are, they generally don't mean a whole lot in real time to me. This one did. I like it a lot when Jesus pops in. I believe the theological word is theophany (eg. Daniel 3:25). It's a rare experience, so when it happens, I'm thinking that I pretty much better listen and listen good. As we say in the kitchen, "Heard!" I rest in the fact that as long as I leave things with Him, my times are in His hands (Psalm 31:15). Several times Paul mentions that we are free men in Christ. Nowadays, His Law is written on our hearts (Jeremiah 31:31-34). Everything is permissible, but not everything is beneficial. (Paul's "Doubtful Things" Romans 14). Freedom is some powerful stuff. Our right to choose empowers the art of love, but the day to day living of it is some tricky territory. I find it's a lot of trial and error. There are some Biblical guidelines, thinking of others first being one that comes to mind, but it can be dicey water. Really it can. This prophetic interlude in my life has left me a bit frazzled. Grateful, but frazzled. Falling back on the traditional teachings of classic thoughts on our faith is looking like a mighty comfortable place to hide under right about now.

Last night was a classic northeast winter night, the rustling leaves and howling wind outside my rattling window was only a minor distraction to the comfiness of being curled up under a pluffy comforter surrounded by mounds of pillows. Reading Luke's Gospel was ice cream on the cake. Becoming a Christian and living alone came simultaneously for me when I was 18. There were a lot of nights that God would have to scare away the crazy monkey in my closet.

A YEAR FOR DAD

My spiritual mentor told me that falling asleep in prayer is like falling asleep in God's arms. Believe it or not, I did that a lot in prison. It usually took a sheet wrapped around my head and two pillows piled on top of me to get there, but those are some sweet memories. I wonder how much of eternity is going to be us cuddled up on God's lap. I was trying to explain my definition of praise to someone the other night. I said, "it's not so much repeating hallelujahyouareworthy over and over again. It's more like, 'Lord, you poked your head right into my history this week. You are awesome!'" I suspect that praise is going to a big part of heaven. Ultimately my decision to *accept the things I do not know* when it comes to tomorrow, is finding great comfort in an eternity of cozy winter nights and recounting those Lord-You're-Awesome moments. I really think what's happening in our lives today has some relevance in forever. I wish the lines weren't so blurry. I wish I could catch a clearer glimpse. Sometimes it's hard to cuddle up to faith. It's all going to make sense, that much I'll be insisting upon.

In the meantime, tomorrow is another day and His mercies are new every morning. Whatever it all means, I'm glad the buck doesn't stop with me. Paul's words in Thessalonians capture a fervent sense of expectancy that, I for one, would genuinely like to catch. HIS KINGDOM IS COMING! One way or another, His kingdom is coming. This is something to **really** look forward to. Today is one more step closer. Like a thief in the night… It's a motivating thought. I'm starting to get excited. I think.

For the Lord Himself will descend from heaven with a shout, with the voice of an archangel,
and with the trumpet of God. And the dead in Christ will rise first. Then we who are alive and
remain, shall be caught up together with them in the clouds to meet the Lord in the air. And thus
we shall always be with the Lord [!]
1 Thessalonions 4: 16, 17

Life Games

The upcoming presidential election has me thinking about change. My son made me laugh when he boiled down the whole thing by passionately asking, "after the last eight years, why *wouldn't* you want a change?" Smart kid. I understand that the basic platform I'm supposed to blindly cling to is pro-life, and then place my ballot accordingly. Problem is, I have a bit of a concern about the whole pro-life stand. I believe that abortion is murder, and therefore wrong, Period. I'm also a realist in that one of the things making abortion illegal would do is to sentence poor silly woman back to the back-alley butchers, without insurance or valid medical care. It's inevitable. I also understand that as long as abortion is legal, we as a society are seemingly condoning the behavior. It's all a bit tricky, really. Should be interesting to see how things go.

I've been sailing along fairly smoothly lately. No huge decisions or milestones to deal with. It's been nice. All of a sudden today, a bunch of serious things have cropped up that had me on my knees. Funny how easy it is for me to chew God's ear off when I need His advice or His help. I realized after about the fourth time today I found myself looking to the sky and trying to leave my worries in His Hands that I hadn't spent near as much time chatting with my triune friends when things were going well. I'm convinced more and more that God's whole desire for us is to be in 24/7 relationship with Him. I'm re-reading, The Shack[15] this week. What an imagination-tickling book. I really do hope heaven is like an old back country farm with a pond full of trout and a waterfall that moistens everything in its path. I can't wait until His presence is in the forefront and a little more tangible. The way things are now, with me stuck in this sin-stained decaying society and Him playing the part of my imaginary friend can be a real struggle. This stuff takes some concentration and discipline. Two words with whom I only have a passing acquaintance.

Unless you've worked in the field, you probably haven't ever given much thought to how a busy restaurant processes, sometimes in excess of over one hundred orders at a time, all the while attempting to maintain the consistency, quality and timeliness of its product. Most bigger restaurants have an Expoditer. The Expoditer is the connection between the front and back, making sure that orders coming from different parts of the kitchen are united for a single table according to the restaurant's and customers specifications. That's all they do. They stand in front of a blazing hot metal shelved window arranging, organizing and co-ordinating. From re-cooks to changed orders, it is the Expo's job to bring it all together. Because the company I work for is so obsessed about food quality and presentation, a Manager functions as the Expo. He's also there to help out the cooks if they get weeded. I expo'd for four years at another restaurant chain, and only occasionally get to do it where I am now. From serving to bartending to front of the house management, my favorite position in the whole restaurant is Expo.

I guess there is a feeling of power, because really, for up to six hours at a time, you hold the experiences of over 100 people in your hands. Staff and guests. And let me tell you, guests can be as insane about the whole thing as staff can be. I often have to remind myself that I'm not performing brain surgery. I don't think that's it though. What I like about *Expoing* is that it's like a life-sized video game to me, where you have to conquer certain tasks and shoot down unexpected asteroids aiming for your head. There is a profound sense of satisfaction when you win a round. That's not to say, you always win. The other reason I love to Expo is because it is like a decision-making-consequence-inflicting microcosm of real life. On a much smaller level, of course. It's like a firing range to practice the art of war, or a mirror-walled studio where dancers figure out their toughest moves. I've learned that no matter what happens you just have to do your best to deal with it, and keep moving. A very snazzy life lesson there.

There's this guy I know. Real old, but looks good for His age. Seems that He had a personal mission to accomplish that would have eternal benefits for a lot of people, but cost Him just about everything. The night before the whole thing was about to go down, He took a couple of His best buddies with Him to watch His back while He took some time to chill. "This sorrow is crushing my life out. Stay here and keep vigil with me." Later, when He went back to check in with them, they were asleep. He was cranky but empathetic, "Can't you stick it out with me a single hour? Stay alert; be in prayer so you don't wander into temptation without even knowing you're in danger. There is a part of you that is eager, ready for anything in God. But there's another part that's as lazy as an old dog sleeping by the fire." Some people say that He was so emotional that He was actually sweating drops of blood. He knew that what was ahead would be painful. He counted the cost. I've also heard it said that He had given one of His most profound chats that night. He must have been exhausted on top of everything else. I don't know how He did it. But He did. "My Father, if there is no other way than this, drinking this cup to the dregs, I'm ready. Do it your way." He was all about His mission, I don't think He had a choice (Matthew 26:38-42).

They say after a while you actually start to appreciate and enjoy things like discipline. Heck, runners claim a high of their own from the endorphin rush. There's another word that at its merest mention I would, in the past, stick my fingers in my ears and start loudly humming the opening song of "The Muppet Show." Surrender. But I have to say that I'm actually growing sort of fond of that little bugger over the last few years. It's actually become a very powerful coping mechanism for me. Time and time again I find myself so very grateful that He never fumbles the ball, no matter how hard I throw it at Him. As scary as change is, I do my darndest to look at it not as an obstacle, but as an opportunity - an opportunity for me to step up to the plate, and hit a homerun. Mostly I'm lucky if I even make contact with the ball. He is always very kind and doesn't laugh at me when I completely miss because I swing the bat like I'm swatting flies. I appreciate that. I shouldn't be surprised that the answer is surrender, it always is. Letting go and letting God be God is all about trusting Him in the most harrowing circumstances. I used to fight it like a crazy man, but I'm learning that turning something over in my brain for hours at a time, or concocting means to my own self-serving end may be more the act of a masochist than a sane person. Sometimes it takes a few false starts, but once things get rolling it becomes another one of those life-games where you get to sit back and watch God do His thing. Watching the way He intricately weaves His ways in to our lives is amazing.

    No doubt, whatever kind of change our Country is about to see, it won't be all that soon. In the meantime, all I can do is trust that God is in His throne, being God.

Shhh, Don't Tell

What is a success? What is a failure? On a scale of 0 – 10; 10 being highly successful and 0 being raspberry-lime jello, I would consider myself a solid 3. Before we get started, let's get the inevitable over with... *success is not measured by earthly ambitions, money or power. Success is living in perfect harmony and surrender to our Lord, Savior Jesus.* Got that. If you factor all of that in then I'd say I'm a big walloping 6. But really, 3.

The obvious question comes up then about my definition of success. I think I've grown a lot in that area. Good looks are nice, but not that important. Money is helpful, and being able to keep my bank balance above 12 cents would be awesome, but really, a vapor. Power is stimulating to the ego, but ultimately pretty shallow. Alive and growing relationship with Jesus: Priceless. (You had to know that was coming.) It's my truth.

I'm struggling. Am I wrong to acknowledge, what I see, as Gods gifts and abilities in myself? One has never accused me of having had an award winning self-esteem, so I don't think so. I'd have to say, my definition of success is more circumstantial than rational. There are these things that I know I can do, that I love to do, that I really think God could use me to do to pitch into the cause, but there is hardly ever any opportunity to use them. To be honest, any opportunity to do what I love to do is a profoundly deep blessing to me. I can't say that I'm not just a little miffed that I don't get to use them more often. I've tried to sell it until the cows come home: that a career in any of the several areas, would benefit the Kingdom, my self-esteem, my wallet, which in turn would translate into less whining coming from me and a more cost-efficient use of the Almighty's time and resources. No sale. In fact, hard as I try, the ringing in my ears gets louder and louder every time the door slams in my face. To add insult to injury, I'm a little disgruntled about those who do get to live to their capacity, not a lot, but every now and then. The "I Can Do That Better" syndrome.

"I Can Do That Better" can be easily remedied with a few words from our sponsor. The Book of Psalms talks about vindication a lot, about how it is wrong to look at someone else's blessings and get jealous. Heck, there's a commandment about it. Envy is never appropriate. 'Get in line' is pretty much the company policy here. I think it's safe to file those feelings under the "Prowls around like a lion seeking whom he can devour." I have a whole trousseau of armor to wage war against the fruits of my humanity if need be.

The gifts thing does bug me. What am I doing wrong? I must be doing something wrong. Now, that thought is good for subtracting a good 4 points from the above mentioned success evaluation scale. Am I *that* off base? It's a definite possibility. How could I be so off? Once again, I need to remember that the problem starts with me. I'm a sinner saved by grace. When push comes to shove, neither myself or my abilities are my own. At times, I find it very comforting to rest in the cliché: God has great things ahead for me. I get a glimmer of hope when someone says that to me. I really want that to be true. I also want the definition of great to mean success, and there is something in me that is tenaciously holding on to that hope. The hope that is certain about something I can't see (Hebrews 11:1). The rest of me, the other 95 percent, the realist bordering on pessimist says, *fuhgedaboutit*. When I can put all that butterfly-in-the-stomach fantasy of success aside, I know that it's a Hebrews12ism about enduring hardship as discipline and what father doesn't discipline his son. I can handle that. I even sorta like that, masochist at heart that I am. Dad's at it again.

I think, deeper down, there's an aspect of shame to it also. It is genuinely my heart of hearts to please my God. I hate that I keep disappointing Him and making a mockery of His kindness. It makes me feel not so great about myself. Shame is a very deep emotion, one that doesn't necessarily have to come from right or wrong. Shame comes from a person' truth. It's pretty heavily guarded territory.

So much of all this seems to demand some kind of learning curve because life is way more of a process than a completed victory. I've got lot's and lot's of time to grow. Eternity in fact. It's hard right now, because I often feel like I'm cramming for a final exam. As frustrating as it can be at times, I'm beginning to cherish His longsuffering. Guess it's one more of those Easter eggs you unexpectedly come upon the morning after Easter is over. Back to basics, God loves me. I think He may even like me; Shhh, don't tell…and check this out:

My head is high, God, held high; I'm looking to you, God;
No hangdog skulking for me.
I've thrown in my lot with you;
You won't embarrass me, will you?
Or let my enemies get the best of me?
Don't embarrass any of us
Who went out on a limb for you.
It's the traitors who should be humiliated.
Show me how you work, God;
School me in your ways.
Take me by the hand;
Lead me down the path of truth.
You are my Savior, aren't you?
Mark the milestones of your mercy and love, God;
Rebuild the ancient landmarks!
Forget that I sowed wild oats;
Mark me with your sign of love.
Plan only the best for me, God!
God is fair and just;
He corrects the misdirected,
Sends them in the right direction.

A YEAR FOR DAD

He gives the rejects his hand,
And leads them step-by-step.
From now on every road you travel
Will take you to God.
Follow the Covenant signs;
Read the charted directions.
Keep up your reputation, God;
Forgive my bad life;
It's been a very bad life.
My question: What are God-worshipers like?
Your answer: Arrows aimed at God's bull's-eye.
They settle down in a promising place;
Their kids inherit a prosperous farm.
God-friendship is for God-worshipers;
They are the ones he confides in.
If I keep my eyes on God,
I won't trip over my own feet.
Look at me and help me!
I'm all alone and in big trouble.
My heart and kidneys are fighting each other;
Call a truce to this civil war.
Take a hard look at my life of hard labor,
Then lift this ton of sin.
Do you see how many people
Have it in for me?
How viciously they hate me?
Keep watch over me and keep me out of trouble;
Don't let me down when I run to you.
Use all your skill to put me together;
I wait to see your finished product.
Psalm 25. THE MESSAGE.

The Price of Admission

I'm feeling a little perturbed. To put it in more spiritual terms, my spirit is grieved. One of the more charming features of the historic area in which I live is a quaint little park only three houses away. In the summer, the neighborhood association gets together and plants all kinds of lovely flowers. It's manicured lawn and plush greenery make it a little like an oasis amidst the crumbling facades of the historic homes surrounding it. During the months of July and August, the park is host to art and music festivals, and community picnics. Today's happening was the annual gay pride event.

Having worked late last night, I awoke this morning to the sound of jazz music playing outside of my window. I decided to check things out. There are usually a lot of cool antiques and booths of local artists, good food and an inspiringly festive spirit. As I got closer, I noticed a bright orange net fencing around the park and a sign that announced the entrance fee of $2.00. Hunh, it was free last year. Then my ears were accosted by the sounds of a passionate voice exploding through a bullhorn. "God loves everyone, even the sinners here today. God so loved the world..." I felt confused. I knew that a lot of my brethren wouldn't approve of me attending such an event, so my first thought was, uh-oh, I've been caught. I stood there for a minute listening to the happy sounds of a live band and revelers singing along dueling with the bullhorn guy. I started to get angry. Also I didn't have $2.00 to spare.

When I got back home something was bugging me about what I'd just experienced. I know that the Church is very vocal about its disdain for homosexuality, and it needs to get a grip about that, but that wasn't it. I am also very aware of the fact that because of where I've been and all I've experienced in my life, I have a far greater tolerance for what is traditionally considered non-acceptable than most. But I couldn't put my finger on it until I took the time to get on my knees and talk it over with Jesus. That's when I realized, I wasn't feeling embarrassed for patronizing a gay pride event, I was embarrassed that as a Christian, I was being represented by the guy with the bullhorn. While the alleged sinners were singing and dancing and enjoying the beauty of the day, my compatriots were expounding judgment, condemnation and dare I say, even hate.

As the salt of the earth and the light of the world, why are Christians characterized by non-believers today as overly-intrusive spoiled sports? Salt and light are normally good things. Born-again Christians are the butt of jokes on late night TV and it's big news when someone in Hollywood "converts." Where did we get the idea that our job is to annoy and scream people into heaven? That's not what Jesus did. He didn't put on a three piece suit and preach hellfire and damnation. He ate, drank and hung out with the sinners. He loved them so much that they wanted what He had to offer. When the woman caught in adultery was about to be stoned, He said, "he who is without sin cast the first stone," and everyone left. Jesus, the only one who had the right to pick up a rock, then offered a word of encouragement and sent her on her way. I fear if that had happened in the park today, she would have walked away with a bullhorn down her throat. The only instance that I can recall where Jesus acted anything like an irate activist was when he drove the money changers out of the temple. They were desecrating His Father's house. He didn't tell them to stop being thieves, He said, don't do it here. On the other hand, several instances of God Incarnate befriending and loving sinners comes to mind. The woman who anointed his head and feet was a prostitute. He had dinner with tax-collectors. He touched lepers and dined with Samaritans. He even died, conquering life and death, next to an insurrectionist.

Church history is a fascinating and incredibly depressing story of misguided behavior in the name of Christ. Thousands were tortured and killed during the Crusades. Forgiveness was sold to build whole cities prior to The Reformation. More recently we've read of buckets of blood being thrown on people walking into abortion clinics and televangelists shaking the faith of millions just for being human. It's no wonder that half of the earth's population thinks we're nuts. In the 17th Century a fella named Galileo was merciless ridiculed and branded a heretic by the church for daring to suggest that the earth was not the center of the universe. A fact we now know to be true today. Shouldn't a movie like "The DaVinci Code"[16] be an opportunity to share truth rather than shove picket signs in people's faces? Am I so afraid to dine with sinners that I have to hide behind a bullhorn? It wasn't those who didn't worship God that Jesus struggled with on so many occasions during His earthly ministry, it was those who thought they were better than everyone else. The religious zealots. The Pharisees.

When I judge someone else and think I'm better than them, even in the simplicity of everyday, I am totally forgetting that it is by grace I have been saved, through faith—and this not from myself, it is the gift of God (Ephesians 2:8). Am I really any better than someone who knows no better than what the world has taught them? If I hope to, in anyway, be a positive influence to those who don't know the power and love of Christ shouldn't, I be making an effort to dine with them, to celebrate the beauty of art or creation with them, to love them sincerely, from a pure heart? I'm angry at myself for allowing that guy with the bullhorn to scare me away because I want, desperately, to show people how much God loves me, a sinner, and how living for Him has given me a hope and security that nothing else in the world could provide. I want to tell them about my friend Jesus, the guy who sticks with me through thick and thin, even when I act like a jerk and make stupid decisions. I want to show them how grateful I am that His mercies are new every morning and that when I mess up He's right there to forgive me and help me not to do it again. I want them to see that they don't have to look high and low or take drugs to find a peace that passes understanding. I want to love them like Jesus. That would have definitely been worth the two bucks.

Tonight I am going to bed with a heavy heart. I missed the gay pride event. I missed an opportunity that may never come again. I'm willing to be ridiculed by the Pharisees of our day. I'm willing to get my hands dirty. The one thing I don't want to do is disappoint my best fried, Jesus. I'm putting $2.00 aside for next year and the next time someone cuts me off on the highway, I'm gonna pray for them. If the teller at the bank makes me wait in line, I'm going to greet her with a smile. If someone needs my coat, I'm going to give it to them, and the next time I see someone thirsty, I'm going to buy them something to drink. You just never know. That drink might be the price of their admission to heaven.

The Price of Admission: One Year Later

A year has gone by and with $2.00 in my pocket, I proudly paid the admission to visit this year's event. The bullhorns hadn't arrived yet, so I strolled the cobblestone paths and checked out some of the booths undaunted. Mostly, my goal was to grab a hotdog because I had no food in my house. Carnival style hotdogs with "the works" are the best.

On my last stroll through the rainbow laden park, I came across a booth that looked like it had some amusing bumperstickers displayed. There were three or four people standing in front of the kiosk, not so much chuckling as in deep thought. The guy behind the table boasted that I would get at least eight laughs per display. I wasn't laughing. Really, no one was. I actually had to read three separate entries before my jaw literally dropped in amazement. I even tried to get behind the humor that might appreciate what I was reading, but I couldn't muster an iota of sympathy. Displayed before me were bulletin boards covered with God/Jesus/Religion-hating stick-ons. Stuff like, "Only idiots believe in Religion," and "God is Nature's way of giving you the finger" and other incredibly offensive ditties like that. It wasn't until I found myself senselessly wandering back toward the hotdog stand that I realized, the bumper sticker booth faces the exact spot that the bullhorn guy would be standing in probably just a few hours. Good strategy.

My first thought was, ok Adam, you played with fire, you got burned. Use the two bux next year and buy some Ring-Dings® and find something else to do. Then I started to get sad. I realized that amidst the merriment, the gaiety if you will, there would be an eviscerating war going on. Not just the one that Paul refers to in Ephesians, "our struggle is not against flesh and blood, but against the rulers, against the authorities, against the powers of this dark world and against the spiritual forces of evil in the heavenly realms," but a real live, blood and guts war of hate. I guess that a world, infected by the ravages of sin, unaware of the very real, and at times, tangible presence of our Creator, would only know one way to wage a war against hate. That would be with hate. Love begets love. Hate begets hate.

So I have to ask myself, 'what are we doing here?!' If Jesus' message were to be boiled down in one word, it would be 'love', right? Right?! Am I missing something? Later that week I ran across a web blog discussing the definition of Christianity. I'd have to pick 'love' again for 500 Alex. God's love is the answer to everyone's question. What am I investing in the world around me? Have I lost sight of the very message God went to an awful lot of trouble to bring? Have I gotten so bored with the simplicity of the Gospel that I'm complicating it with my lists of rights and wrongs and to-do's? Why has it never occurred to me until now that this world was in such a state of lostness that God had to cut through all of the ceremonial confusion, not with more rules and regulations, but with a clean slate engraved with one very simple word. Love. When Jesus was asked what the greatest command was. Love. For what reason did He claim He came (John 3:16)? Love. What was one of His greatest concerns as he hung suffocating on the cross that He asked Hisis good buddy to handle for Him? Love. The Gospel in a word is love.

I went back to the park later in the day. I wanted to commend the three little old nuns that had a "Jesus Loves You" booth set up right in between glass blown figurines and the practice safe sex displays. I felt better knowing that while I was having my little spiritual tantrum, God had the park covered. I also didn't want to not-love a bunch of people who Jesus might have planned to touch that day.

After it was all over, I sat on my front stoop as people packed up their booths and went home. I told God that I wasn't going to let one person pass without trying to reach out even with a simple "beautiful day". Some people stopped and chatted, some just nodded back, a rather unattractive drag queen decided to take the first step and have a cigarette with me after commenting about the agony of wearing six inch heals all day. I told him what I would tell any woman who said the same thing: sneakers are comfy and cheap. I had a lot of fun. I discussed the bumper sticker booth with a bunch of different people that afternoon and none of them were too thrilled about it. I even got to tell them my theory about how hate begets hate and love begets love.

Why is it so hard to get it through my head that love is what its supposed to be all about. That He is weaving His love, grace and generosity throughout my life every waking moment. All of my guilt, and shame and remorse and self-flagellation are just detours to the war that is being fought around me. I don't need a ministry to call my own. I don't need my words printed in a book. I just need to experience Christ's love so intimately in my heart that, regardless of my flaws and weaknesses, it flows through even in the simplest "Have a good day."

I think I got my $2.00 worth this year; the hotdog was top notch, I coveted some beautiful ceramic pieces and now I see that the war of hate is being fought from both sides. It makes me sad. Even more so, it makes me angry. Why would anyone "pick-a-war?" Seems we Christians have been doing it for Centuries. When sermons use war metaphors to speak of outsiders, haven't we forgotten who the enemy truly is? I'm bummed again because what I really need to do is start back at square one and lovingly apologize for the stains of my humanity, and let people know how much more precious God's unconditional love is to me because I'm such a hot mess. We are all sinners, saved by grace. Loved by God. Admission is free.

In The Twinkle of An Eye

I love the story Brennan Manning tells in his book, Ruthless Trust[17] of a 4 year old boy who falls in a lake. His Dad, after three dives to the bottom, finds him clinging at the bottom to the post of an old pier. After prying his sons fingers loose from the stanchion and dragging him ashore, "his father asks, "Billy, what were you doing down there?" The little one replied, "Just waitin' on you Dad, just waitin' on you." That's me, holding my breath, under gallons of mistakes and their very real repercussions, trusting with all of my heart that my Dad in heaven is rescuing me and I will one day joyfully bask in His glory. Just waitin' on you Dad.

I like getting older. I always have. I like the memories and experiences I've had, the people I've met, the places I've been. Sure there are days of my life that I wish I could re-live, things I could fix, maybe some hearts I wish I could unbreak. Honestly, without the *what I know now* stuff, I wouldn't re-live my life again for all the tea in China. Nor would I know what to do with all the tea in China. There would probably be a whole country of angry people if I had all of China's tea. I can't see any good angle to a deal like that at all. I'm becoming more and more convinced that somehow when this is all over it's all going to fit together like the delicate stitches of Oriental embroidery. Right now, it seems like a kitten's tangled mess.

Time can be an odd task master. Whether I believe in God's intimate involvement in my life, or whether I think that as long as I don't cuss, go to Church, don't smoke weed or have lustful thoughts everything is A-O-K really matters very little. God's truth is God's truth. What I believe about my Heavenly Father doesn't change God, it changes me. Unfortunately, the only arena that I have right now to experience the presence of the Almighty in my life is in this Creation infected by sin that I live in. Even the scientists will agree, we are on the decline, although they may see the source as more physical than spiritual, it's a fact. And like another one of those Easter Eggs that appear out of know where, I understand now that having an Earthly Father was originally intended as a gift. Not a gift like getting a new walkman. It was more like the batteries that are disappointingly wrapped separately that you open with a resounding, "Oh yeah, guess I'll need some batteries for that thing." Problem is, a lot of us got batteries without a lot of juice. Some of us didn't get any batteries at all. There is a whole soundtrack to life that most of us are barely hearing because we got defective batteries. Blessed is he who's EverReadys® are fully charged.

A few months ago, my brother announced to me that he had officially lived longer than our Dad. It was a big deal to him. It would be to me too. When I was little, "Dad" was a fellow of mythical proportion. It was a startling fact when I realized, that though weighted with potential, and intended as a very generous security blanket from my Father above, Dad was a guy, just like me.

I don't know that there is any right way to end a collection of thoughts and life-lessons because, frankly, only God has the ability to write the very last chapter. However, as I read and re-read the lessons that God has been teaching me I'm excited to see some growth. The rest is a work in progress. What has come from the experience of sharing a year with Dad is a deeper understanding of our Heavenly Father's purposes. If I have one gripe with The Big Guy, it's that this whole thing is so danged confusing. Society is littered with people who live as their own God and then there is the other side who believe that Puritanical enforcement of holiness is the Gospel's only message. It's hard to find a place for those of us who love God but are chronically infected with the 21st Century. Who find little to no use for traditions and regulations. Folks who want to get back to basics without compromise. Yet the Bible teaches that we are the ones His heart rejoices in the most. The questioners. The doubters. The angry ones. We need to let God to be who He really is, not some pre-defined puppet confined to a man-made theological box with his name carved in a first row pew. We are the rebels of the faith, the apple-cart turneroverers, and that has left the list-makers frustrated, and angry. Christians have turned Jesus' message of love into a religion in which you tow the party line or be cast off as a pariah. Jesus spent a lot of time swimming with the pariahs of His day, and He loved each and every one of them for exactly who and where they were. Over and over again I read about Jesus going against the religious grain, trying to bring back into focus that which religiosity had so confused. Jesus was a man who lived on the edge.

I am one of society's outcasts, but God loves me all the same. His daily gifts to me can't be measured in bank accounts or success or fame. It is the reality of His all encompassing forgiveness, His grace, His mercy and ultimately His love that hold me fast. I'm tired of the confusion. The confusion that each and every one of us bring to the topic of God. Christianity is an exhausting journey. But at least for me, hanging out with Christ is like being granted hinds feet to climb high places and taking deep gulps of refreshing mountain air. He's my Dawg.

One day I want to gather a bunch of "nonbelievers" together and tell them a story, one of my *lots of adjectives* stories. The only prerequisite would be that the hearers must accept the facts as true, whether they inwardly believe them to be or not. I would talk about a benevolent Being who created a species so that He could enjoy them and they could enjoy Him. How just one act of defiance broke the intimate trust that had existed between man and God and hurt His heart deeply. But as wounded as God was He still made provisions for them. He kept His original promises and led His miserable band of misfits right into The Promised Land. Then I would talk about religion and greed and thirst for power and how God's heart must have been so very grieved that his creations tried to shrink His benevolence down into a formula. I would talk about how He jumped right in to history, just at the right time, and forgave thousands of years of sin by becoming one of His own creations and sacrificing His life for the forgiveness of the world. I'd talk about Pentecost and the Holy Spirit's creative involvement in our lives.

Eventually the story would return to corruption and the devastation that was caused by Eve's disobedience in the garden. How that sin has grown from generation to generation and that the whole thing has become like a dirty smelly fish tank. One that God faithfully and carefully immerses His hand in to protect those He made. Those He loves. I would talk about how Jesus provided Him free access to get His hands all gunky and wet for us and how one day, He promises to replace the filter system completely, kill all the algae and let us swim in waters so crystal clear that even the Almighty will take a dip with us.

If even only one person in the group could see how much sense it makes. It's not so hard to see how cloudy the waters we live in are or how frantically God is feeling His way around the tank to work with us. He is trying so hard to save our souls from the very sickness that has everyone so discombobulated that no one really knows where they are going. When my Dad left this earth, I believe that my Heavenly Father felt a pang in His heart as well, and for whatever reason chose to reveal Himself to me, in a way that no matter how hard I tried I couldn't get around. I hate that the waters of my life have been so slimy and rough, but I cherish every second that He was there, holding my hand, working it all out for the good.

One day I hope to get to meet my biological Dad again, though the circumstances I can't even begin to imagine. In the meantime, another year has come and gone and each day is a challenge to follow God's unique path for me. I'm sorry to all the people in my life to whom I've represented Christ so poorly; please don't base you opinion of God's benevolence on me. The water seems to get cloudier every day.

A YEAR FOR DAD

Thousands of years is a long time for a people to hold on to a hope that seems to have less and less meaning. Yet God's Word has proven its reliability and accuracy for every one of those years. Whether it be by physical death or The Glorious Appearing, we will all face the reality one day that God so loved the world that He gave His only begotten Son...

Dad, you will never be far from me, but I'm moving on. Whatever part in the play you had has been finished for so long. Your baby boy has grown up and I just know that when the day comes that I stand nose to nose before my God, there will be a twinkle in His smile that I haven't seen for years. A glimmer that I recall reflecting in your azure blue eyes. We really are created in our Father's image and I can't wait to see you again in Him. Thank you Dad for giving me life, and thank you Father for making it so adventurous and abundant. Thanks too for chocolate.

NOTES & FOOTNOTES

[1] Donald Miller, *Searching For God Knows What* (Nashville, TN, Thomas Nelson, 2004)
Miller's amazing and insightful words helped me to gather and contain thoughts that had spilled through my brain over the last few years. He specifically uses the Chernobyl reference and filling the inner hole references mentioned here.

[2] Max Lucado, *A Gentle Thunder* (Nashville, TN, Thomas Nelson, 1995)
Having read this book in jail, I can't provide the exact page, however, contained within is an interlude of prose so moving that the first few times I read it I was brought to tears. It is the story of Creation – Lucado style. It is a song of God's lov, and profoundly addresses the fact that making man with free will was a dangerous but unavoidable risk on the part if our Creator.

[3] Frank E. Peretti, *This Present Darkness* (Wheaton, IL, Crossway Books, 2003).
Peretti's novels often depict parallel views of what's going on in the world as we know it and then intersperses glimpses in to the spiritual realm. Some of the good vs. evil conflicts are depicted quite graphically.

[4] G.D. Watson (1845-1924), "Others May, You Cannot"

[5] "Who Am I" Mark Hall / Stephen Curtis Chapman, Producer. Album: *Casting Crowns* (Nashville TN, Beach Street Records, 2003).

[6] "I Can Only Imagine" Bert Miller / Pete Kipley, Producer. Album: *Almost There* (Nashville, TN, INO Records, 2001).

[7] "My Heart Will Go On", Celine Dion / James Horner, Will Hennings. Album: *Titanic: Music from the Motion Picture* (New York, NY, Sony Classical, 1997).

[8] "Cat's In The Cradle", Harry & Sandra Chapman. Album: *Verities & Balderdash.* (Los Angeles, CA, Elektra Records, 1974)

[9] Elizabeth Scott: "Benefits of Forgiveness" www.stress.about.com/od/relationships/a/forgiveness.htm. (March, 2008)

[10] Bradford & Grant, Vinette Caroll "Your Arms Are Too Short to Box With God" (New York, NY, Eugene O'Neill Theatre. 1976)

[11] Wikipedia Online Encyclopedia: "Lucid Dreams" http://en.wikipedia.org/wiki/Conscious_dream. (May, 2004)

[12] Oswald Chambers, *My Utmost For His Highest* (Grand Rapids MI, Dodd & Mead Co., 1935
Specifically, the devotional entry for March 20th

[13] Rob Bell, *Vevet Elvis* (Grand Rapids, MI, Zondervan, 2005)
Bell addresses several important issues that all of us, as followers of Christ, should address. The concept of an evolving Christianity is specifically timely and the author's knowledge of Jewish culture enriches his treatise to greater levels of understanding of basic concepts.

[14] "How Great Thou Art" written by Carl Gustav Boberg (1859–1940)."

How Great Thou Art is a Christian hymn based on a Swedish poem popularized by George Beverly Shea and Cliff Barrows during Billy Graham crusades.

[15] William P. Young *The Shack* (Newbury Park, CA, Windblown Media. 2007).

[16] Dan Brown, *The DaVinci Code* (New York, NY, Doubleday Books. 2003).

[17] Brennan Manning *Ruthless Trust* (San Francisco, CA, HarperCollins Books, 2000).

THANKS & ACKNOWLEGEMENTS

To be honest, I don't feel a lot of connection to Whomever put these words together, so Spirit, thanks for letting me put my name on it. And, of course the rest of you guys in the Trinity - y'all are always my inspiration. Without You and The Word, I would probably be spinning in circles in the middle of a highway out in no-where, wearing only pair of argyle boxer briefs a cowboy hat and singing show tunes.

I have a great deal of gratitude for everyone I've met along the way, because they have all had an impact on who God has made me today. There are of course the specific standouts: Mom, Dad, Brig, Robby, Liz, Curt, Chris, Ashley, Gabe, Debbie, Aunt Bob, Babci & Anne. With love.

Then there are those who, more currently seem to be God's emissaries at times for inspiration, or just a swift kick in the butt: Lizzie, my spiritual Mom, Here's to the road we never took. My, Graceful Steph (and annoyingly consistent proofreader), Michael, My own personal angel., My Life-Advisor and dear friend, Julie, One Stop John, OB 3919, Joe C. at MHA, GE… These are people who have helped to infuse some of my crazy with a bit of sanity when the synapses start misfiring all over the place. And Chris, really, these curses usually have a shelf date. 'I hope you dance'. One day Ash, one day. You will always be my Peanut. Thanks to your Angel too. Forever & Always.

So often through this project I sat back thinking about how truly narcissistic the whole journal-essay concept is. Who cares about the life of a guy like me? And every time I wanted to throw in the towel, two songs would pop-up. *Who Am I* by Casting Crowns, and *I can Only Imagine* by Mercy Me. (I also have a very special place in my heart for *So Long Self*.) Thanks to all you guys; the ministry of an artist is a challenge I can't even fathom. I discovered current contemporary spiritual music, (prior to which my repertoire consisted of strictly Michael W. Smith, and Amy Grant) during my last year in prison through a station called K-LOVE. They are a great ministry (www.klove.com). Nowadays I listen to them almost everyday streaming online. One day, I gotta send them a testimonial, and some money.

Last but not least, to you, thanks for reading. Really, if you've gotten this far, you probably realize that the Dad thing, though certainly a cathartic parenthesis around the actual essays, is a cavern in my heart that I very rarely venture to deeply within nowadays. I've discovered, it's not because it's too painful, but more out of resignation. 33 years is a long time. It does crop up when I notice the parallels between the subtle messages I learned from him during the 14 1/2 years he was around when they conflict with real-life truths about my heavenly Father. It can be maddening, and confusing. Somehow too I am living with the very real symptoms of Bipolar Affective Disorder and Borderline Personality Disorder. Meds tend to block creativity, mania sometimes feels good and the latter BPD can make you act and look like a real horse's arse sometimes. As far as the Father image thing goes, it is something we all have to deal with, and God being God will, in His time, turn it in to a blessing.

Today there are kids out there who badly need positive male role models. **The Mentoring Project** does an amazing work. (www.thementoringproject.org). I wish I could have been involved with something like that at that age. Donald Miller's writings have been so inspiring to me that I want to say thank you, for helping me sort through a million random thoughts and make them coagulate in to something almost intelligible. His *Blue Like Jazz* should be mandatory reading for everyone who is trying to make heads or tails out of the God that organized religion has left us with. Special thanks too for the mental smacks in the head too from Rob Bell, Brennan Manning, Anne Lamotte, Melody Green, Frank Peretti, Janet Evanovich and John Grisham.

Late at night, when it's just me, my pillow, the cat and God, I sometimes wonder if I'm just making the whole thing up; believing some fairytale that was concocted 2000 years ago by a bunch of drunken shepherds after a night of pillaging. Christianity has historically thwarted, in some pretty gruesome ways, the advancement of technology and civilization. So if it's all a myth, it's a pretty powerful one. Then there is the calm, rational voice of truth that eases my racing heart and nurtures a sense of gratitude and awe that fills me head to toe. There is a lot that doesn't make sense. God can be as frustrating as He can be loving and protective. It really should come as no surprise that my humanity cannot comprehend the workings of a Being that I believe to be so much bigger than anyone gives Him credit for. When I open my Bible and I sense a wave of peace run through my veins, or when I pray at a level so gut deep that it physically hurts to stop crying, not to mention those little Easter Eggs hidden all over the place, I know that what I'm dealing with here goes way beyond mythical proportions. It's all very real. Jesus, The Holy Spirit, the whole shebang. The time has come to be accountable to society and everyone who has had a church door slam in their face, or a sword brought to their throat. Religianity doesn't work anymore. Corporate religion never did. God is after the core of our beings; He wants our hearts. And He wants to give us His. By us, I mean you, me, Aunt Tessie, Uncle Clem, each and every spirit that he lovingly created and hand-stamped with His own image. He longs to fellowship with us individually and intimately. Why some of us see that and others don't is another mystery to me. I am however, so very grateful for the path He has chosen for me And for His loving me even when I least deserve it. I am especially grateful the word "deserve" isn't even in His vocabulary.

Adam is available for speaking engagements, regardless of the size.
You can contact him directly at:

adamhadflz@gmail.com
or
819 Centre Ave.
Reading, Pa. 19601

http://ayearfordad.com

Always glad fort feedback!